THE ECHOES OF HER HEART

THE HEART OF A WOMAN,
HER LORD & HER LIFE.

ALETHEA AWUKU

Copyright © 2018 by Alethea Awuku

The Echoes of Her Heart
The heart of a woman, her Lord & her life

All rights reserved under international copyright law. This book may not be copied or reproduced in whole or part in any form without the written consent of the author. The use of quotations or irregular page copying for personal use is allowed and encouraged.

ISBN: 978-1-5272-2679-1
Publisher Name: The Echoes of Her Heart Publishing
United Kingdom

Scripture quotations are taken from the New King James Version®. Copyright © 1982 by Thomas Nelson. Used by permission. All rights reserved

THE ECHOES OF HER HEART

THE HEART OF A WOMAN,
HER LORD & HER LIFE.

May the Lord meet you in the pages of this book as He unveils the layers of your heart.

Lots of love, Alethea A

ACKNOWLEDGEMENTS

To my Lord, who is continually doing a great work in my own heart each and every day.

To Stanley Awuku, my wonderful husband. Thank you for planting the seed in my heart to write this book. I doubt it would be here if you did not encourage me to see the bigger picture of *being a vessel for God's glory*.

Contents

INTRODUCTION   *xi*

PART 1: THE BEGINNING

  1. Who am I?
     The Echoes of My Heart: Journal entry   *23*
  2. Who are you?
     Misplaced identity   *27*
  3. Who you really are   *49*

PART 2: THE ENTRANCE OF SIN

  4. The Distortion   *73*
  5. The Fall   *77*

PART 3: A MATTER OF THE HEART

  6. The desire of the heart   *89*
  7. The function of the heart   *95*
  8. The purpose of the heart
     God, the relationship initiator   *107*
  9. A captivating beauty   *127*

PART 4: BROKENNESS

  10. A sacred pain   *141*
  11. Sacred abandonment   *153*
  12. A strange fruit   *159*
  13. A deceitful heart   *171*

14. Beautifully broken   *179*

PART 5: AN UNVEILED HEART

15. A sensitive heart   *195*
16. A circumcised heart   *203*
17. A resolved heart   *211*
18. A call to holiness   *221*
19. A restored, whole and healed heart   *231*

INTRODUCTION

The Echo of *her* heart
The Echo of *my* heart
The Echo of *your* heart

Every woman's *heart* has an echo. An echo, which continuously thrums and reverberates to the rhythmic beat of our deepest thoughts, silent prayers, feelings, questions, desires, fears, and doubts – all of which are present at different seasons and stages of our lives. My mention of *heart* does not refer to our physical hearts, but is used as a spiritual metaphor to describe the inner part of us that no one sees. It is linked to our spirit and our soul (which comprises the mind/conscience, will and emotions) - the core of our being, and who we are as women.

If there is one thing that I have grown acutely aware of as a woman, it is the *ever-changing* state of my own heart – its sinful tendencies (unbelief, greed and unforgiveness, just to name a few), and its ability to be a powerful driving force in my life. I am keenly aware that no matter how nicely I attempt to dress and present myself outwardly, at my very core, I am sin-sick and deeply flawed.

I am in desperate need of the wonderful grace, love and mercy that my redeeming God offers, and how thankful I am for this!

Our hearts are very important to God. This inner part of us is what Jesus was concerned about when He said to the

Pharisees:

Brood of vipers! How can you, being evil, speak good things? For out of the abundance of the heart the mouth speaks. A good man out of the good treasure of his heart brings forth good things, and an evil man out of the evil treasure brings forth evil things.

- MATTHEW 12:34-35

And elsewhere:

For out of the heart proceed evil thoughts, murders, adulteries, fornications, thefts, false witness, blasphemies.

- MATTHEW 15:19

Here, we see that the heart is found to be at the root of all things, and our language, thoughts and behaviour are its fruit. Our heart's potential to influence us must never be underestimated.

The heart brings forth all manner of things, and unless it is transformed, our lives will never experience reformation. Without submitting to a diligent, intentional, and disciplined study of our lives in light of God's Word, and without truly encountering the holiness of God, the Holy Spirit is not given the opportunity to illumine truth into our hearts, in order for us to see ourselves for who we really are.

The discussion concerning womanhood - particularly God's directives for biblical womanhood - can be difficult to examine corporately and embrace personally in our modern world. I know I have had my fair share of wrestling matches with God in my attempt to understand His purpose behind our creation and existence! The prevailing dominance of the feminist movement, which champions women's supposed choice and liberation from masculine authority, has done untold damage to women.

Feminism was birthed in the 18th century out of an awakening to see women rightly acknowledged with equal worth, value and respect to men in political, economic, personal, and social spheres. What began as an earnest desire to receive appropriate recognition and appreciation very quickly became a vehicle used to aggressively wage war, overtly and insidiously, against God's purposeful design for men and women.

I can distinctly remember the *battle of the sexes* wars that went on during my time in school. *Gosh, he is just so slow. What's wrong with guys?* My friend casually said to me one day in class. Now, we were not really educated in the area of feminism, but even at a young age, we girls had quickly concluded that *boys were dumb and slow,* and we were *smart and bright.* Even if there were a more articulate and evidence-based way to express this, our attitudes at such a tender age were distorted and unhealthy! When our identity rests in our gender, we will feel the compulsion to engage with feminism and gender equality, being quick to criticise traditional roles and functions of women.

From Genesis 1:27, we see how *God created man in His own image; in the image of God He created him; male and female He created them.* In His original design, God did not create women to be less valuable than men. This is also affirmed in Paul's New Testament teachings such as Galatians 3:28, where he states:

> *There is neither Jew nor Greek, there is neither slave nor free, there is neither male nor female; for you are all one in*

Christ Jesus.

Here we see that great dignity is given to both genders, as they work and co-exist in oneness in God – a beautiful reflection of the relationship within the Godhead itself.

In the account of Jesus and the Samaritan woman (John 4), we see an example of Jesus boldly resisting a culture that considered women to be second-class by not only engaging in a loving dialogue with a woman at a water well, but offering her salvation - *true spiritual nourishment that would satisfy her thirst for the rest of her days.* It is the entrance of Sin that caused men to mistreat and misunderstand the value of women, and women to devalue the role and place of men.

The feminist message has unfortunately permeated every sphere of our lives – from our careers and relationships, to homemaking, seeking to challenge God's created order and to set women on a path that is independent from the Creator's original and good design. The hope was that this ideology would enable women to find true fulfilment, purpose, and balance in their lives. However, if we are very honest, the added alternatives and opportunities have brought on more stress and responsibility, which can be even more difficult to balance!

The fundamental subject of womanhood cannot be explored or even uncovered by looking at humanity, or by women picking up placards and marching for their equal rights before God, their communities and nations.

To understand the significance of womanhood, we must firstly embrace the truth that it was never God's intention for women to be in competition with men. We see this in Genesis 2:18 – in the very beginning *before* the creation of Eve:

And the LORD God said, "It is not good that man should be alone; I will make him a helper comparable to him."

Do you notice something astounding here? God created woman not to be *identical* to a man, but *comparable* to him – a complimentary opposite. This suggests that woman was created as the perfect counterpart for man – neither inferior nor superior, but alike and equal to him in her personhood, while distinct and unique in her function.

She, too, is significant.

God could have created another male friend as a companion for Adam, but He decided otherwise. The woman was in His plans, and she was to be created with specific requirements and purpose. Her role and function, along with Adam's, would be a pattern set for future generations to follow. How glorious!

The subject of womanhood, therefore, can only be explored by reverentially and transparently approaching God's biblical directives to mankind and specifically, to women. We must desire to hear God's instructions well, accept them and begin to apply them to our lives by His grace. In seeking to know the purpose of our very design and composition, we ought to ask honest questions such as:

Why were we created female?
Why, as women, do we think the way we do?
What is our significance and purpose?
How can we flourish in all that God has created us to be and do?

These questions, directed to a loving God, will ultimately lead us to uncover a marvellous, Christ-glorifying, countercultural truth that we can explore, embrace and begin to contently live out.

So, what about the consideration of the inner heart? Well, to what can I liken a woman becoming awakened to a life that is Christ-focused and free from worldly distortion and distraction? Perhaps it is the picture of true grace, strength, wisdom, love, and meekness. When a woman enters into a covenantal relationship with God through the Lord Jesus Christ, her life is spiritually fortified because He becomes the foundation upon which all else is built. She gains clarity concerning her worth, value, identity and place in the world and His Kingdom. She need not look elsewhere for answers, validation, affirmation and purpose.

It goes without saying, then, that through all the changing scenes of life, God must be the anchor by which our hearts and lives are grounded. It is our heart that He desires to rule over and awaken to the knowledge of Himself, and it is my sincere prayer that as we begin or continue our journey with Him, we reach the place where we genuinely find ourselves surrendering our *entire* hearts to Him.

Everything originates from the state and condition of the heart. Whatever we ingest mentally, physically, emotionally and spiritually changes us inwardly and results in our behaviour and speech. The heart is the very chamber that God has always desired of mankind, and as we see in Deuteronomy 6:5, His command is that *You shall love the Lord your God with all your heart, with all your soul, and with all your strength.* This calls for total abandonment of the self to a loving and powerful God.

From the book of Genesis, we see how an almighty, transcendent, self-sufficient, holy and magnificent God created man to have an intimate and covenantal relationship with Him. His instruction and treatment of people has always been with the intention of making it known that His desire was and still is to dwell *within* their lives.

The Old Testament prophets such as Moses, Jeremiah, Isaiah, Habakkuk, Hosea, Amos and Joel were all used by God to paint vivid images and relay messages to the people of Israel of God's eagerness for them to abandon the world and hold fast to Him. We consistently see this in the husbandry language used to express God's covenant love for Israel:

For your Maker is your husband, The LORD of hosts is His name; And your Redeemer is the Holy One of Israel; He is called the God of the whole earth.

- ISAIAH 54:5

Israel's rebellion towards God signalled how hardened their hearts were towards Him.

The New Testament ushered in a new covenant between God and mankind. When Jesus came to this earth, He was the Word made flesh (John 1:14), demonstrating in a new way God's intent to personally dwell with man, full of grace and love. Jesus Christ spent considerable time teaching and demonstrating that God's desire was not for us to outwardly perform and conform to legalistic Laws. In the Old Testament, the Laws were put into place to act as a mirror, showing the Israelites how sinful they were, and that they could not meet God's requirements in their own ability. God also put the Laws in place to point to a deeper spiritual truth – their need for a Saviour and Mediator, which would be revealed and fulfilled in the New Testament through Jesus Christ.

In seeking to ritually observe the Laws, both Jews and Gentiles alike were placing the directive letter of the Law above the spirit of the Law (the deeper spiritual meaning behind the Law's instruction, which was the awakening and conversion of the heart to totally love God out of willingness and not duty). When I think of this, I am reminded that true faith is a precious gift, originating from an inward revelation of who God is, and what He has done for us through His Son Jesus Christ. Faith is not produced by the striving of our human effort to produce works, nor is it sustained by our feeble attempt to please God in order to feel good about ourselves.

Certainly, many of us may fall into the temptation of believing that we must present our works to God as a necessary condition for His love and acceptance to flow towards us. We may be able to convince ourselves that our works are first a demonstration of faith; however, without a penetrative understanding of the proper purpose and place of our works, we very easily become preoccupied with an adherence to moral Law, rather than a loving desire to yield to the leading and transformative work of the Holy Spirit in our lives. It is much easier to put on a performance out of religious duty and self-righteousness, and be distracted by that which *looks* spiritual – I have seen this so many times in my own life. However, Jesus' parables and teachings point to the condition of the heart above our actions.

Several thousands of years have gone by, and here we are, recipients of the Gospel in our age. God's message and desire to dwell within us has not changed. The Gospel of Jesus Christ is unrelenting in seeking to convert every single area of our hearts, and indeed, it is completely and powerfully able to do so. God must have every part of our lives. Having half of us simply will not do, and as a woman, there are many areas of my life where I need God's wisdom and guidance. In the following pages, we will explore the various areas of our hearts, looking at the Fall and what it has done to the heart of a woman; the purpose and function of our hearts; brokenness; and aspects of an unveiled, healed and restored heart.

Writing this book has confronted and continues to confront my own heart, its deepest fears and its many shortcomings. It has caused me to share and reflect upon many of my own personal experiences. I give glory to God for that because it helps me to remain humble and to seek Him for daily grace, wisdom and sanctification. This book will not be an easy read for some, and you may need to re-read certain sections in order to glean your own revelation and *wow* moments from these pages. That is a good thing.

Take your time with this book. In seeking to mature and bloom beautifully, we must have a thirst for biblical knowledge, revelation and understanding. We must resist the urge to coast on the surface of several of the real issues that we women face. It is my hope that within these pages, you will find some elements from my heart that speak deeply and truthfully to your own heart, and you will be encouraged to take the time to study and explore further, so that you may know yourself and, most importantly, your God, ever more deeply.

PART 1
THE BEGINNING

"O God, I have tasted Thy goodness, and it has both satisfied me and made me thirsty for more. I am painfully conscious of my need for further grace. I am ashamed of my lack of desire. O God, the Triune God, I want to want Thee; I long to be filled with longing; I thirst to be made more thirsty still. Show me Thy glory; I pray Thee, so that I may know Thee indeed. Begin in mercy a new work of love within me. Say to my soul, 'Rise up my love, my fair one, and come away.' Then give me grace to rise and follow Thee up from this misty lowland where I have wandered so long."

– **A.W. Tozer** - The Pursuit of God.

1.
WHO AM I?

The Echoes of My Heart: Journal Entry

Dear Lord,

Who am I? What a strange and peculiar question to ask oneself. On one hand, it seems a little farcical and harsh to interrogate myself in such a way. However, upon serious thought of this question, I have come to realise that perhaps I am afraid of such a question! I find myself instinctively giving in to the overwhelming temptation to flippantly gloss over this question with peripheral answers such as, "I am unique; I enjoy reading and writing," rather than boldly approaching and wrestling with the complex layers that reside within and make up what is known to be my heart and the very fabric of my being.

The question, "Who am I?" is one of the most important questions that I can ask myself as a growing woman in an ever-changing world. This question is a catalyst. It causes several chain reactions, which ultimately lead me to You. I thought that I knew who I was, until one day I realised that the reflection in the mirror was a hollow composition, a construction of other people's words, thoughts and lives. Suddenly, Lord, everything around me fell away. It all crumbled beneath my very feet, and I could do nothing but watch as the rubble receded from my view. In light of this invasive question, "Who am I?", everything evaporates.

My heart is screaming, "Lord! I thought that my identity was safe and secure in the things and the people around me."

If not that, then I thought that my identity was defined in the things that I could buy and possess and even if that failed, then at least I could #girlboss it out and find the security that I needed in myself. I now realise that I do myself a serious disservice and injustice when I do not allow the deep ache within my heart to draw me to You. Oh, how my heart aches.

I ache for someone to know me, to seek after me and to never let me go. I ache for something otherworldly – something that I cannot quite touch or explain, but that my soul knows very well.

Where does this capacity come from? I know that my feeble mind cannot contain it. You see my frame. You know my frame, and so it is to You that I come to find out who I really am, and what I was created for. Uncover the layers of my heart, Lord. There is much beauty, yearning, resistance and waywardness within me. Teach me and show me who I am.

[EXCERPT TAKEN FROM MY JOURNAL]

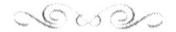

The consecrated Christian life is often portrayed as stifling and old fashioned, and if we are honest with ourselves, we may have felt this at one time or another. Sometimes the grass appears to be greener on the other side. But that's just the thing – it is an appearance.

2.
WHO ARE YOU?
Misplaced Identity

Do you know who you are? God made you a woman. Accept His gift. Don't be afraid to be feminine and to add physical and spiritual loveliness to the setting where He has placed you. You are a child of God. You are a part of the bride of Christ. You belong to the King – you are royalty. Dress and conduct yourself in a way that reflects your high and holy calling. God has called you out of this world's system – don't let the world press you into its mold. Don't think, dress, or act like the world; inwardly and outwardly, let others see the difference He makes in your life.

–Nancy Leigh DeMoss - Lies Women Believe: And the Truth that Sets Them Free.

You can often spot her from a mile away. This young woman is overconfident and loves to be the centre of attention. The scent of her perfume is domineering, her clothes too tight, excessive or inappropriate for the occasion, and her hair and clothing carefully constructed to fit in with the hair fad or fashion of the moment. She must learn and display the latest dance moves and sayings of the times, and appears to have a 'don't mess with me' attitude. Perhaps she even has a group of girlfriends who are similar to her. Who is she seeking to impress? Well, we aren't entirely sure yet. This young woman is outwardly beautiful, and she knows it. She is confident, sassy and witty, yet deep down she desires to be known for more than her looks. Her beauty has become her choice of weapon, her safe place, her greatest attribute and the only feature that she feels confident in. *This lady has a problem.*

Then there's the other candidate. This young woman is reserved and does *not* possess the courage to say that she wants to be the centre of attention. However, secretly, she longs to be the centre of everyone's conversation and thoughts because she desires the validation that such knowledge and feeling provides her. She may dress awkwardly at times, wishing that she owned all the latest and best clothing. Externally, she may not be the one the opposite sex gawks at, or the one that all her female friends wish they could be like, and deep down, this bothers her. This young woman has a desire to be outwardly beautiful to others and may spend a lot of her time admiring the confidence, sass and beauty of other women. At times, she feels frustrated because she finds that she has to strive to have what candidate A has, as it doesn't come naturally to her. *This lady also has a problem.*

Although the two descriptions above are very generalised, indulge me for a moment. *What is the problem, and what do these two beautiful women have in common?* Typically, they are both searching and striving for something that is elusive in the physical and has its root in the spiritual. *In some way, does this not reflect our own lives, as we often strive to satisfy our spiritual and emotional aches through physical means?*

For these two women, their striving is typically characterised by a crafting of their outward looks and an inner desire that stretches and challenges their present reality. What they desire is deeper than an outward projection, and yet this outward projection seems to be the only means of helping them communicate how they feel. They both have a distorted view of *who they are*. Does this remind you of a friend you know? Does it resonate with *your own* experience in any way?

***

I possessed a type of beauty that I forcibly and superficially constructed from the world:
Trying so hard to fit in, I was blinded to the truth that it was elusive, and I never truly owned it or believed it.
The knowledge of Your love has set me free from that trap, and in being awakened to YOU,
I have known a different type of love and beauty.
I actually don't have any beauty of my own.
Your beauty, Lord, is one that transcends what I see; it is rooted and springs forth from the spiritual to find itself in beautiful bursts and fragrances in various areas of my life.
It exudes elegance and is clothed in much grace.
I could think of 100 ways and reasons to denounce this beauty on my worst days,
but I cannot deny it because my soul KNOWS it.
Quite frankly, I am beautiful because you say so and in YOU I have been created to be so.

[EXCERPT TAKEN FROM MY JOURNAL]

***

I can vividly remember searching for a sense of stability during my teenage years and early twenties. My own experience bears more of a resemblance to the second lady described. I struggled greatly in the area of beauty and fashion, never quite sensing that I had reached the status of *cool, desired and popular* among my peers. I placed a considerable amount of worth in my physical appearance and would regularly feel a sense of shame when I didn't measure up to the standards of beauty presented on the television and around me.

As this went unchecked, I developed a complex of being awkward, introverted and feeling alien compared to those who I perceived to be *normal*. Deep within, I knew that I was more than my looks; however, I had no courage to appropriate this knowledge to my life. I hated how I felt but didn't know the cause of it, and I also didn't know how to escape from it.

I grew well acquainted with tears and would often find myself embarrassingly caught off guard by how quickly and frequently they would make their appearance – *often at the most inappropriate times* when I was with friends and having casual conversations.

Yes, I was that girl who wore a huge mask, in my feeble attempt to cover up the mess that lay within. A huge part of me didn't want to claim that the mess was mine. Because after all, I *couldn't possibly* be a deeply insecure and unrooted young woman who didn't actually know what was going on within her own heart. I wrestled daily with my pride as it successfully kept me in a state of pretence, closed off from seeking support. Yet there was another overwhelming desire within, beckoning me to just exhale *and let all the mess leak out of me.*

I believed that I was unwanted, and that there was nothing in me to be desired. Thankfully, God is so gracious and so kind and the mask wasn't to stay on for very long. I soon discovered that when I would try to put the mask on, my mess would somehow find a way to seep through the edges and cracks to make itself known. I knew that something deeper and bigger was calling me to begin an inward work before concerning myself with the outward, and it wasn't until I had an encounter with Jesus Christ that I finally began to walk the path of understanding my value, purpose and identity.

I wasn't shamed into freedom.

Rather, God showed me who He was, and who I was *in Him*. Gradually, over time, the layers of distorted thinking were shed until, together, we got to the core of my hidden person. I began to grow roots into the most beautiful One.

The hidden person of the heart – your character, your integrity and your spirit – is indestructible and incorruptible according to 1 Peter 3. This person doesn't fade away and is the very thing that moulds and prepares our hearts as God's dwelling place. When I realised this, my focus shifted away from myself toward desiring to grow to reflect more of Christ.

MISPLACED FOCUS

I am not sure if men do this as much, or in a different way, but have you noticed that when women meet, we tend to fall into the habit of instantly checking one another from head to toe as we make our assumptions and judgements, drawing conclusions about the other person's life story, career status, personality and the like.

Yet outward perception and looks do not necessarily marry up with the thoughts that individuals have of themselves. The examples of the two women previously mentioned, and my own experience, demonstrate a common and familiar desire found in so many women. When we possess a deep longing (a gaping void that can only be filled by a relationship with God), we are often very quick to attempt satisfying it with an unhealthy preoccupation with ourselves, other people, material objects and experiences, because we have knowledge that they will bring us some degree of happiness and comfort, albeit fleeting. *Have you ever experienced this in your own life?*

Without a shadow of a doubt, most women have experienced this in some shape or form and because of this, one of the most difficult things for us can be to draw near to God with all of our struggles, weaknesses and failings before we really hit rock bottom. Although He invites us every single day to come to Him, when our hearts are filled and focused on the attainment of worldly aspirations and pursuits, there isn't enough room for the Lord to dwell in our hearts as He would desire to.

'GODS' OVER GOD

The first time I heard the words *idols* and *fake gods*, it was summer, and I was 16. I remember the day clearly, as if it were just yesterday. There was a special programme scheduled for the youth of the church at our annual retreat. It was a warm, sun-filled afternoon, and we all gathered in the hall after lunch – a little begrudgingly because we wanted to stay outside. After a short introduction from our youth leader, we watched a video by an American preacher sharing a message about the music industry and its negative effects on the minds of the young generation.

Some of the *cool* ones seemed untouched by the message, but for the most part, we were all hooked. Never in my life had I been so convicted, rebuked, enlightened and encouraged to consecrate my life to Jesus! The message cut straight into my heart, compelling me to examine my whole life with an x-ray to identify the areas of excessive attention to unhealthy things.

I couldn't believe that I had allowed so much into my heart. I returned home after the retreat with such a strong desire to get rid of all the idols that I knew were interfering with my desire for Christ. I destroyed all of my CD's, took down all the celebrity posters on my wall and cleared my room of all my worldly magazines. I began to understand more about the detrimental effects of idols and people-worship, and I knew that Jesus needed to have my whole heart.

When it comes to this area of idols, getting rid of the things that lead us to develop unhealthy habits is good and necessary. For many of us, it is usually the first step to decluttering physically and emotionally – like the shedding of old skin to reveal the new. However, what I have learned over the years is that it's just not enough to declutter. We must go a step further to *de-own* – teaching, disciplining and nurturing the heart to let go of the things and people that we have allowed to occupy a significant part of our hearts *unchallenged.*

A god is described as *any person or thing to which excessive attention is given.* It may seem a little extreme to describe the things that we give attention to as our gods, but at the heart of this description is the excessive and self-indulgent inclination that we can have towards material living, gadgets, possessions and the people around us. If you think about what consumes your time and energy every single day, upon close examination you cannot help but notice how that thing or person has shaped your life, or is currently doing so.

Our early years are typically characterised by a clambering and desperate search for significance, stability, value and identity as we try to make sense of our lives and purpose within our world. In doing so, we naturally tend to latch onto the people and things that we perceive to provide anchorage for our lives before we have even encountered God. As a result, our families and friends, the media and other things form the foundations that influence and shape our thinking and inculcate certain attitudes in us. They can, and often do become the *gods* that receive much of our affection.

Perhaps if you think back to your own childhood and teenage years, or even your life now, you may be able to identify the things or people that have contributed significantly to giving your life meaning and context. Perhaps you can recall some television shows, music videos, pop artists and personal life experiences that have held great value in your life and defined your earlier years. As I realised at that church retreat, all of these things point to pillars of influence in our lives.

As a result of this and the continuing process of socialisation, we are often under the compulsion to subconsciously *search* for a place or person to fasten our value and worth to, in order to feel a sense of purpose and certainty. Perhaps your current reality draws from someone else's outrageous, scandalous lifestyle because it is sexy, daring, bold and speaks loudly and intensely to a part of you that desires this for yourself. All of these influences project a particular ideology, and in doing so, they create expectations and form the foundations and building blocks for what we perceive life to be like, and how we fit into it.

Sole dependence upon all of these avenues, while ignoring Christ, creates a distorted perception of life. In His Word, and through a personal revelation and relationship with Him, He shows us that He is *the true source* to which our lives must be anchored and rooted. Therefore, without a right understanding of our relationship with God, we can spend a lot of time, energy and resources on things that don't adequately feed our spiritual lives.

As women, our chief desires therefore must be to:
1. Acquire personal knowledge and love towards God who has created us.
2. Understand *what* God has created us for and *why* He has created us as we are.

Without approaching and bridging these two points, we fall prey to misplaced identity. It therefore goes without saying that if you are here, living and breathing, God has created you for a specific purpose, which is still unfolding with each passing day. Our struggle often lies in the fact that we find it difficult to open our hearts to respond to God's invitation to walk with us, fill us and help us embark on the journey toward full spiritual maturity, love and knowledge of His person. Yet it is only when we first know Him that we can begin to know ourselves and emerge as the women that He created us to be.

It isn't a secret that advertising and marketing heavily saturate our lives. Due to many external influences, we are often full and stuffed to the brim with other gods in the form of celebrities, social media, material possessions and the preoccupation with a culture that only promotes the pursuit of self. God has given us the freedom to enjoy ourselves here on this earth; however, with freedom also comes responsibility. When we become so absorbed with earthly things, we become *one with them,* and that was never God's intention. I am reminded of Colossians 3:1-3 which encourages us to set our affections on the things above, and not on the earth.

Incorrectly handling earthly possessions and people, as well as idolising popular culture, could effectively mean that we grant them the authority to displace God and hijack the most precious place that belongs to Him: *our hearts*. In this regard, Christian women have been called to be very different indeed, embracing and living out countercultural, biblical truths in a world that is cold and distant toward God. God has called us into an intimate covenantal relationship, and anything that we idolise becomes adultery against our Bridegroom. I love the following quote by author Elisabeth Elliot:

> *The fact that I am a woman does not make me a different*

kind of Christian, but the fact that I am a Christian makes me a different kind of woman.

This means that as Christian women, we have been called to a different standard and pursuit in Jesus Christ. It means that our awareness, movements, roles, function and realities as women aren't to be guided by the things of this world, but by the inner and tangible voice of Jesus Christ, with whom we have a relationship.

When a woman turns material possessions or people into her gods, she encounters a serious problem. In seeking to discover who she truly is, she may well find herself entangled (sometimes through no fault of her own) in an overbearing web of influence, which mercilessly pulls her in every direction. Without understanding who she is in Christ, she is left vulnerable to survey everywhere for answers, rather than considering the Word of God – her Owner's manual and blueprint for her life. Walking with God in an intimate relationship is the great emancipator of our souls, yet we often overlook Him in our pursuit of fruitless remedies for our aching and questioning hearts.

The most fascinating thing about external gods is that although our lives are so saturated and influenced by them, they do not provide lasting satisfaction and fulfilment. You may have realised by now that material possessions, pursuits of this world and other people cannot fulfil the deep cravings of your soul. Of course, temporarily, they provide an incredibly exciting high. However, the appetite that you and I have is too big – *too deep* to be contained by the things of this earth. After all our energy has been spent in the pursuit of these gods, we may well find ourselves echoing the very same words as King Solomon:

All things are full of labor; Man cannot express it. The eye is not satisfied with seeing, Nor the ear filled with hearing.

- ECCLESIASTES 1:8

In other words, *is that it? What's next?*

External gods create an even bigger void in our hearts when we realise that in and of themselves, they hold no great value; they cannot satisfy what our hearts truly long for and were created for. Even ultimate pleasure and achieving all earthly goals has an element of futility, as Solomon laments:

I said in my heart, "Come now, I will test you with mirth; therefore enjoy pleasure"; but surely, this also was vanity. I said of laughter— "Madness!"; and of mirth, "What does it accomplish?" I searched in my heart how to gratify my flesh with wine, while guiding my heart with wisdom, and how to lay hold on folly, till I might see what was good for the sons of men to do under heaven all the days of their lives.

I made my works great, I built myself houses, and planted myself vineyards. I made myself gardens and orchards, and I planted all kinds of fruit trees in them. I made myself water pools from which to water the growing trees of the grove. I acquired male and female servants, and had servants born in my house. Yes, I had greater possessions of herds and flocks than all who were in Jerusalem before me. I also gathered for myself silver and gold and the special treasures of kings and of the provinces. I acquired male and female singers, the delights of the sons of men, and musical instruments of all kinds. So I became great and excelled more than all who were before me in Jerusalem. Also my wisdom remained with me.

Whatever my eyes desired I did not keep from them. I did not withhold my heart from any pleasure, For my heart rejoiced in all my labor; And this was my reward from all my labor. Then I looked on all the works that my hands had done

And on the labor in which I had toiled; And indeed all was vanity and grasping for the wind. There was no profit under the sun.

- ECCLESIASTES 2:1-11

When I first read this passage of Scripture, I thought to myself, *Well, what's the point in doing anything, God, if it's all meaningless?!* It can all sound a little dreary when you look around and think that everything you spend so much time working and living for is *vanity, has no profit under the sun* and will turn into a big heap of ashes one day.

Yet, if you read between the lines of what Solomon is saying, you'll notice that this passage really speaks of an incredible hope. Although everything as we know it is destined to pass away (including all the debt, bills and cleaning-*hurrah!*), there is a greater cause and purpose for which our lives were created.

A glorious eternity with Jesus awaits us.

All that we labour for on earth is perishable, and if you are like me, you may also be tempted to ask, *how should I feel about all my earthly goals, dreams and achievements then?* Matthew 6:19-21 encourages us to use a large portion of our time and resources laying treasures up in heaven. Christ is our treasure, and we can earnestly dig and seek to find Him in our everyday lives. When we find Him, we receive the strength to not only get through our days on earth and enjoy them, but most importantly, we keep heaven in view, and our lives are built up from our knowledge of this.

Everything we invest in our heavenly accounts is sure to be kept safely without rot or rust. If you look closely, you will notice that Jesus doesn't actually preach about money itself being evil. It is simply perishable, like everything else. What He focused on was the state of our hearts *concerning* earthly things (1 Timothy 6:10). An obsessive attitude towards material things can cause our hearts to rot long before our possessions perish.

The heart is always the issue.

And He said to them, "Take heed and beware of covetousness, for one's life does not consist in the abundance of the things he possesses." Then He spoke a parable to them, saying: "The ground of a certain rich man yielded plentifully. And he thought within himself, saying, 'What shall I do, since I have no room to store my crops?' So, he said, 'I will do this: I will pull down my barns and build greater, and there I will store all my crops and my goods. And I will say to my soul, "Soul, you have many goods laid up for many years; take your ease; eat, drink, and be merry."' But God said to him, 'Fool! This night your soul will be required of you; then whose will those things be which you have provided?' "So is he who lays up treasure for himself and is not rich toward God."

- LUKE 12:15-21

One's life does not consist in the abundance of the things he possesses. This is so contrary to the message we often hear today. There is a great richness that is infused into the life of a soul that knows its maker is God, and lives unto Him. So, as we go about in life, enjoying material things, we ought to remember that we must not dig our roots into them, but be content to keep our hearts upon Jesus Christ.

The movie *Love Finds You in Charm* tells the story of a young Amish woman who wasn't content with what she felt to be her small, very sheltered world. After seeing a life of supposed *freedom* outside of her own, and while reading Jane Austin's *Pride and Prejudice,* she began to restlessly long for adventure and travel in the outside world. She visited a cousin for the summer, and while there, she was exposed to a fast-paced, exciting world – all that she had longed for, and very different from her quiet, religious life.

Soon, her story reaches a point where she must choose which life she wants to live and after experiencing both sides, she surprisingly chose to go *back* to her Amish life.

The film spoke volumes to my own soul that has from time to time longed for *a carefree, fun* life that other people appear to have. *Have you ever felt this in your own soul?* This lady thought that everything she wanted was in the world, until she had a taste of it and realised that it wasn't sufficient to satisfy her.

Rather than feeling embarrassed for having such a desire in the first place, she relished the fact that she had learned an important lesson of *valuing* her portion in life. She confidently stood up and turned her back on the world because it wasn't for her, and there was nothing truly valuable in it. She quickly realised that her Christian values and beliefs stood in stark contrast to those of the world and so turned back to her faith-filled life with renewed strength and conviction. May I add that she also found love with a handsome Amish man? *The dream.*

This film holds a special place in my heart because it speaks so intensely to what most of us women experience on a daily basis. The consecrated Christian life is often portrayed as stifling and old fashioned and if we are honest with ourselves, we may have *felt* this at one time or another. Sometimes the grass appears to be greener on the other side. But that's just the thing – it is an *appearance*.

When we see others travelling, purchasing nice things and celebrating constantly, we can be tempted to feel like the fun is *over there*. The truth is, whatever you cultivate, water and tend to will grow, and with Christ in it, there is *lasting* nourishment. So be content with your portion and relish the gift of the Christian life.

Popular media often projects idealistic and exaggerated lifestyles that set the woman off on a pursuit of attaining all or parts of this goal in the hope that doing so will provide her life with greater significance and meaning. However, this can further deepen our ache when we realise that it is nothing but a smokescreen designed to entice us to simply spend our money. We may be left feeling disappointed and betrayed because we put all of our value and worth into one basket, hoping that it would yield results, only to be left feeling even more inadequate than before.

Despite this, many of us may still become so entangled in the lies that we have been fed that we can find ourselves struggling to totally break free from them. When we give other things and people such authority over our lives, they increase in capacity and dominance, and the more they increase, the less we will feel motivated to respond to God, let alone desire to live a life patterned after His leading.

THE EXCHANGE

...and changed the glory of the incorruptible God into an image made like corruptible man—and birds and four-footed animals and creeping things.

- ROMANS 1:23

The road leading to compromise is a deadly one, for it turns what was once a heart aflame for God into a dim and cool one. Once we make the decision to ignore God, we fall into the trap of believing everything else, as well as attempting to make gods out of cheap figurines, other objects, and people. We see this so vividly in Exodus 32 when the Israelites demanded a golden calf (a cult idol) be built during Moses' absence, when he went up to Mount Sinai to seek the Lord's face. Although physically, they had been released from their bondage to the Egyptians, inwardly, they had not been converted and they didn't have an intimate relationship with God. This led to great compromise and idol worship.

This indicates that we were created with the purpose and propensity to worship, and without our gaze upon Jesus, we will very quickly exchange our worship to Him for less worthy, more convenient and temporary objects.

Can you identify this exchange in your own life? Somewhere along our life's journey, there have been moments where we have traded in the soul-nourishing knowledge and experience of God for *cheap figurines,* only to come to the realisation that nothing can fulfil us like communion with and abiding in Jesus Christ.

Our identity does not come from the world, and a woman who is not diligent and intentional in her efforts toward Christ will soon find herself striving to pattern her life after this world and its *gods*, aspiring to lay hold of the often-elusive, mirage-like lifestyles that are advertised to appear real.

The value of a woman must not be diminished or overlooked because:
1. We have an identity of our own – in Jesus Christ.
2. We are worth knowing deeply – in Jesus Christ.
3. What we find will not be perfect, but we mustn't be afraid of what and who we will uncover in Him.

Therefore, we must:
1. Invest time and energy in knowing who Jesus Christ is.
2. Ask God to help us cultivate the *desire* and interest to know who He has made us to be in Him.

Lady, do you know who you are apart from your worldly possessions, achievements, family, and friends? The Lord prompted this very question within my own aching and searching heart, and it caused me to pause and reflect. We won't find the answers to the deep questions of our hearts in the culture that we live in because it is far too distorted; nor will we find them within ourselves, because our experiences are too limited. We won't even find all the answers to our questions from our own mothers or female mentors, because many of them, like us, are still on their own journey and are learning everyday just as we are. God awakens an inquisitive questioning within our hearts when He wants us to search after the answers *in Him.*

Take some time to think about this question: *Do you know who you are apart from your worldly possessions, achievements, family, and friends?* Write down the thoughts that come to mind. True change occurs when we point the flashlight into our own hearts, and earnestly seek after change. Reflect on it, pray about it, and let God begin to unravel the layers of who you really are to you.

There may be areas of your own life that have been compromised, and as such, have left you questioning who you are and what you have been created for. Letting go of artificial gods allows the Gospel message to truly permeate our hearts and cause everlasting internal change. *Will I let it?* This is the question to ask yourself.

THE ECHOES OF *YOUR* HEART

- *Can you identify any gods in your own life? Where did they come from?*
- *Can you identify and reflect on the things or people that are a current or have been a historical influence in your life?*
- *Can you think of people who you have modelled your life after? What about their life was appealing to you? Why?*
- *Is it possible that God wants you to look at your life with Him with fresh eyes? Where are the ways that you can see this?*
- *Do you have a friend who you can encourage with this information?*

A CALL TO ACTION

Some ways that we can be more intentional in our relationship with Christ:

- Consider the things that are currently distracting you. Perhaps you could look at reducing the time

spent on those things?
- Begin a regular Bible study. You can begin by reading a particular book or by looking at a particular topic, such as *God's love*. We are creatures of habit, and if we set a time and place for meeting with God daily, we are much more likely to honour it. Don't forget your study tools (Bible, reading plan, journal, pen).
- Begin a regular prayer time with God. The Bible encourages us to cast our burdens upon Him (Psalm 55:22). We can go to God with our cares and needs and sit before Him to hear what He has to say to us each day!
- Begin journaling. When you study or pray, have a journal nearby to record what God says to you or any thoughts that come to mind. Journaling helps us to remain focused on God. You can also read through your journal at a later stage to be reminded of something God has taught you or brought you through. If you don't have a journal, you can purchase a faith-based one at:
www.theechoesofherheart.com
- Commit to memorising Scripture as it is a great help in guarding, comforting and instructing our hearts as we do life, all the while reminding us of God's precious promises.

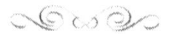

God created women in His image and likeness to reflect His glory, and if He is a spirit, it means that the essence of who we really are is spirit, not flesh.

3.
WHO YOU REALLY ARE

What exactly is a True Woman? She is, quite simply, a woman who is being molded and shaped according to God's design. She's a woman who loves Jesus and whose life is grounded in, tethered to and enabled by Christ and His Gospel. As a result, she is serious about bringing her thoughts and actions in line with what the Bible says about who she is and how she ought to live. She is a woman who rejects the world's pattern for womanhood, and gladly wears God's designer label instead.

–**Mary A. Kassian** - True Woman 101: Divine Design: An Eight-Week Study on Biblical Womanhood

A TESTIMONY OF ABOUNDING GRACE, MERCY AND LOVE

In the quiet of the morning as I got ready for university, I suddenly found myself staring back at my reflection in the long, rectangular mirror. I wasn't quite sure who or what I was looking at. *Is this what I look like – I mean, really look like?* My inquiring eyes traced the edges of my round, brown face – my nose, forehead, mouth and chin. I looked at my shiny, black, straight limp hair – a result of several painful relaxers. *I am definitely an African woman. I am a female.* I edged closer to the mirror, creating a little bit of a mist with my breath. *But what does that mean?*

I edged a little closer again and quieted my mind enough to sense my own heartbeat. Staring at myself for this long was making me feel a little weird, and I hadn't even performed a whole-body scan yet. I didn't like it, and yet, I wanted to know more. I wanted to know what lay behind my dark, brown eyes and the rest of my external frame. *Who would I find?* As quickly as I was able to quiet my mind, it was soon flooded with several questions about what was looking back at me in the mirror. I longed to understand how I fit into the world. *Am I acceptable?*

I had questions and a deep ache that needed to be uprooted.

I promptly got myself together and moved on with my morning as though I hadn't just had a strange encounter with myself. Yet deep down, there existed a *knowing* that there was more to me than what my skin colour, culture, interests and heritage presented. Although I attended a church fellowship, I had no relationship with the Christ who I so professed my love to. So, when this ache would present itself, I defaulted to the only outlet I had grown to believe was normal: seeking the attention of boys.

Due to popular media, peer influence and other means of exposure, most young girls encounter the world of sex and relationships at a very young age, and it was no different for me. What was marginally unconventional in my experience is that for some reason, my relationships did not involve any physical intimacy. What was more prevalent in my experience was the emotional disarray within my own heart: a direct reflection of a heart that had not yet found its home in God.

When God does not rule over our hearts, we misunderstand

and misdirect our desires toward *created things*. In my experience, the root of my misdirection was my lack of knowledge of God, coupled with deep emotional insecurities. I *fell in love* quickly, and often, giving my heart away to any guy who would express *any* desire in me. I spent countless hours wishing I was somebody else other than myself, and as you can imagine, a lot of time nursing my wounded heart, only to fall back into the experience of giving it away again.

Later spiritual growth in the Lord highlighted the root of this ache, and I came face-to-face with God's words to me.

You have prostituted your heart and given yourself away cheaply, Alethea.

Huh?

When most people think of prostitution, they may immediately think of women selling their bodies to any interested man for a price. In my case, my heart was what was being prostituted, and its currency? Male attention. I had not learned nor cultivated the truth within myself that my *value, worth, purpose and significance* are tethered to *Christ alone*. Consequently, considerable time was spent foolishly *misapplying* my worth and value to immature males who needed development themselves.

I settled for whoever gave me attention. Although I knew the experience would be fleeting and fictitious at best, I still yearned to drink deeply of the initial high the male attention gave me. In those transient moments, it felt easier to ignore that inner tug for lasting satisfaction. However, just like a narcotic, when the attention wore off, I would be left again in a state of anguish, desperate for the next fix. I dangerously and falsely believed that my yearning was a license to give my heart away. I didn't understand love. How could I when I did not even know the One who *was* Love? Therefore, what I gave and received was an incomplete and counterfeit version of it.

Can you relate?

Developing deep-seated, obsessive and unhealthy emotional ties to other people or objects desecrates and defiles the altar of the heart, which is a place that must only be reserved for God, and upon which pure worship is to be offered to Him. Strongholds that bind us to another instead of God alter the state of the heart, causing it to embrace and pursue deceit and forgery as though it were truth. The only way to break the chains of emotional strongholds is through the washing, deliverance and healing that the Gospel brings.

However, just hearing the Gospel is not always sufficient, as we see in the following passages:

But be doers of the word, and not hearers only, deceiving yourselves. For if anyone is a hearer of the word and not a doer, he is like a man observing his natural face in a mirror; for he observes himself, goes away, and immediately forgets what kind of man he was. But he who looks into the perfect law of liberty and continues in it, and is not a forgetful hearer but a doer of the work, this one will be blessed in what he does.

- JAMES 1:22-25

"Therefore whoever hears these sayings of Mine, and does them, I will liken him to a wise man who built his house on the rock: and the rain descended, the floods came, and the winds blew and beat on that house; and it did not fall, for it was founded on the rock. "But everyone who hears these sayings of Mine, and does not do them, will be like a foolish man who built his house on the sand: and the rain descended, the floods came, and the winds blew and beat on that house; and it fell. And great was its fall."

- MATTHEW 7:24-27

There must be a revelation and embedding of God's truth in our hearts, and then an active *putting into practice* for true freedom to pierce through the dark thick fog of misunderstanding and misdirection.

Without a true knowledge and awakening within the heart of the Holy One, we cannot aspire toward the holy life that He alone offers us. We certainly cannot develop the yearning and discipline that is needed to embrace God's truth and reject the lies of the world. There must be a complete filling within a woman's heart with the Lord, lest the lure of the world takes over and lays an unsteady and faltering foundation upon which no lasting house can be built.

The day finally came when the scales fell from *my* eyes and the Lord placed a spiritual mirror before me. At last, I could see my true reflection. I was extremely rough around the edges – *in fact, I was jagged* and a true sinner who had been giving herself away to the world, rather than responding to the One in Whom her identity was to be found. I saw my brokenness and rebellion, as well as paradoxically how innocuous I was, not in my pursuit of happiness, but in my pursuit of personal wholeness and true meaning in life.

Many years of erroneous belief had led me on a futile pursuit of nothing but emptiness. I came face to face with God, and He gripped and compelled my tired, tender heart toward repentance. Surrendering to the Lord was my only path toward achieving the wholeness which I so desperately needed and searched for.

There is much beauty in surrender. It causes an illumining within the heart toward the things that it once overlooked. Here I suddenly was, awakening to the truth of the real Gospel - that God was drawing, tugging and knocking at the door of my heart for me to fully respond to Him in love. He was jealous for me and desired to fill every part of me with Himself. His mercy hung over me, dripped in love, forgiveness and redemption.

This began my true journey, not toward self-discovery, but toward *God discovery,* through intimate study of His Word. The Gospel message is simply stunning, and when we begin to sense its power to rescue us from a futile way of living, we are able to gladly accept God's invitation to be with Him. How wonderful is that? The Bible is many things, but chiefly it is God's open love letter to us, because in it, we receive knowledge, wisdom, strength, hope and most importantly, the faith to persevere through all circumstances in this life. Many deep-seated insecurities and uncertainties are resolved when a woman begins to explore and understand who she really is in the Lord. What a gracious, merciful and loving God He is in making Himself available to us!

Behold, I stand at the door and knock, if anyone hears My voice and opens the door, I will come in to him and dine with him, and he with Me.

- REVELATION 3:20

KNOWING WHO WE REALLY ARE BEGINS WITH THE GOSPEL

The Gospel is all encompassing. It is, in fact, the only source of godliness. Search anywhere else, and you have nothing more than self-reform at best, and idolatry at its worst.

–Barbara Hughes – Disciplines of a godly woman

A changed heart begins with hearing and wholly embracing the Gospel of Jesus Christ, and I am persuaded that this Gospel is sufficient for all who believe, enabling us to live victorious and transformed lives in God. It is important for women to know what the Gospel is, what it means for us, believe it wholeheartedly and by the grace of God, live it out daily.

My journey to discovering who I was began when I accepted that the Gospel is not what I think or manufacture it to be, but it is founded upon God's perspective; it reveals who God says He is, who God says we are with and without Him, and His promises and dealings with humanity. Once we understand this and truly receive it into our hearts, we must then be prepared for its application, seeking to make it the centre of our lives. This is the only way we will witness its transforming power.

In our pride and desire for self-sufficiency, it is easy to believe that we don't need to be changed because we have bitten into the lie that in and of ourselves, we are enough. To compound this belief, there are messages from the pulpit that tell us that we are beautiful and worthy in every way. While this is not a terrible or necessarily incorrect message, such teachings are often partially presented or taught out of context. In seeking to encourage, they can actually lead us onto a path of pomposity and vanity.

Certainly, we are valuable, worthy and incredibly significant to God; however, to understand our true value and worth, we must firstly look at this in context of who God is, who we are without Him and what He has done for us. Only when we look at it from this perspective can we begin to see that without Christ, we are wretched, wayward and unworthy. It is He who makes us worthy by His loving exchange.

For He made Him who knew no sin to be sin for us, that we might become the righteousness of God in Him.

- 2 CORINTHIANS 5:21

When we accept Jesus Christ into our hearts, it is essentially an acceptance of adoption into His royal family. Our poverty and lack are exchanged for His riches, and the blessings, wisdom and inheritance that belong to Christ also become ours, *not* because we have done anything to earn or deserve them, but because these privileges are bestowed upon us by virtue of adoption and sonship.

The Gospel first begins with God who, in His abounding love and mercy for mankind, sent Jesus Christ to die on the cross to redeem us back to Himself, despite our being unworthy of this love and mercy. Our failure to associate our value to the work of the cross can set us on a path of distortion, littered with self-righteous works. In order to truly appreciate who we are in Christ, we must come face to face with our unrighteous, disobedient, rebellious and sinful hearts, and in doing so, be struck with a humble and true recognition of our depraved state. This causes us to repent before the Lord and desire that He change us to reflect His image and live for Him.

To constantly receive messages telling us that we are

enough all by ourselves only inflates our egos and causes us to glorify ourselves above God. Apart from Christ, we are under the wrath of God, deserving just punishment because of sin that separates us from Him. Without Christ, we are unholy and unclean before a holy God, and that is why our redemption by the blood of Jesus Christ is so important. Through this, we stand justified and at peace with God (Romans 5:1-2). The true Gospel cuts deep into the sinner's heart, revealing what is really there. Dear lady, do you see that you are made righteous and worthy *because of* Christ?

The Gospel shapes everything about our identity and purpose, and must empower and motivate us to live every day of our lives for Jesus. So many of us ask the question *who am I?* Within the pages of the Bible, we learn some powerful, fundamental truths about who we are in Jesus Christ that can set us all on the journey toward true liberty! We do not need to walk around with an identity crisis or complex, and we certainly do not need to feel forgotten, invaluable or worthless.

It is my prayer that as we attempt to unpack this question together within this chapter, it awakens something spectacular within you that will cause you to desire to explore and know more.

It is firstly important to note that though we can commune with God through conversation, dance and song, He is a spirit. Genesis 1:26-27 tells us what God said about *us* in the very beginning:

Then God said, "Let Us make man in Our image, according to Our likeness; let them have dominion over the fish of the sea, over the birds of the air, and over the cattle, over all the earth and over every creeping thing that creeps on the earth." So God created man in His own image; in the image of God He created him; male and female He created them.

God created women in His image and likeness to reflect His glory, and if He is a spirit, it means that the *essence* of who we really are is *spirit*, not flesh. Our spirit lives in an earthly body – a tent, as the apostle Paul mentions in 2 Corinthians 5:1, and we have a soul, which comprises of our will, emotions and intellect. There is no higher dignity than to know that the essence of who we are is *spirit*, patterned after the God of the universe!

Being made in the spiritual *likeness* of God means that we are a direct reflection of His very nature and complexity. This is incredibly significant. It means that the occasional or perpetual sensing of *something more* within our hearts is very much legitimate, as there indeed is more to us than the physical realm displays. Therefore, all of our questioning and exploration must begin *in spirit – with God*, and not through earthly means. Material things can make us feel and look good, and elevate us to a particular status in society, but they can't confirm to us what our real identities are.

You are a spiritual being, made in the image of God in order to walk in an intimate relationship with Him, serve and glorify Him on this earth and forever in eternity. By true repentance, a sinner is united with Jesus Christ through His timeless, selfless, efficacious sacrifice on the cross. This union means that through no effort of our own, we become co-heirs with Christ, possessing eternal blessings in God (Ephesians 1). Having this incredible opportunity means that we lay down our old lives for the new, grace-filled, and Holy Spirit-powered life offered to us. This enables us to be light- and image-bearers of God within our homes, communities and world. *That is your dignity, your meaning, identity and destiny.*

Let's keep going...

- **In our earthly experience, we have been made distinctly female, and it is to the glory of God. We have been created with great care, dignity, intricacy and purpose.**

According to the dictionary, *femininity (also called womanliness or womanhood) is a set of attributes, behaviours and roles generally associated with girls and women. Femininity is partially socially constructed, but made up of both socially defined and biologically created factors.*

Behavioural traits generally considered to be feminine include gentleness, empathy and sensitivity, though traits associated with femininity vary depending on location and context and include a variety of social and cultural factors.

The list is exhaustive. In God's creativity, all women are different in personality, strengths and attributes.

The first thing to note here is that God did not make us men. He made us distinctly and uniquely female. There is great purpose behind this, and there is great significance to this. We must resist the contrary, popular trend, which suggests that although God designed us, He may have been confused about whether we were actually meant to be male. In your experience, you may have found that your femininity or womanhood is defined by and therefore subservient to what popular culture dictates and approves of. In many ways, we all have grown to embrace this, as generally, society upholds and celebrates particular female icons and messages to us.

We may even find ourselves drawing inspiration and information of what a true woman is 'supposed' to be from culture. However, without a biblical foundation, culture does not provide true understanding of what God created a woman to be. The Bible says in Psalm 139:13-16:

For You formed my inward parts; You covered me in my mother's womb. I will praise You, for I am fearfully and wonderfully made; Marvelous are Your works, And that my soul knows very well. My frame was not hidden from You, When I was made in secret, And skillfully wrought in the lowest parts of the earth. Your eyes saw my substance, being yet unformed. And in Your book they all were written, The days fashioned for me, When as yet there were none of them.

God, who created our very frame, knows us deeply and intimately. He knows every detail of our lives, every hair upon our heads, our feelings, thoughts, and inclinations. So many of us yearn to be known deeply by a significant other. To be seen, celebrated and valued for what is within is an unspoken yet overwhelming desire within many of our hearts. In the passage above, the Psalmist is thanking and praising God who knows Him so intimately. This same God also knows us in the exact same way.

We have been given the mandate to purposefully champion biblical femininity, and we must do our best to protect womanhood as the Bible defines and expresses it. What is presented in the Bible is not archaic and outdated, as some would suggest. Rather, what lies there is true freedom, fulfilment and purpose for every woman. A woman who proudly wears the label of biblical womanhood seeks to walk in the pattern that was set for her by her Creator. Her resolve concerning this demonstrates that she was fearfully and wonderfully made.

We live in a culture that cares little for this, preferring to dilute and eradicate the message of biblical femininity. When we look at Genesis 1, we see the significance that was placed on the woman's existence, role and function. After God had created the earth as well as Adam, something was still missing – the woman. She was not an afterthought, but a crowning glory – the missing piece to the jigsaw puzzle that would make the picture complete.

Being distinctly female was never something to be lived out in shame or resentment. We live in a world that now seeks to blend the boundaries between male and female, but part of understanding who we are in God is accepting that in His wisdom, He created us to be women. God intended that we would relate to Him in this way as Creator and Father, and live out the love story of Christ and His Church with our male counterparts in marriage, if that be part of our story (Ephesians 5:22-31). Being a woman is a gift to our homes, relationships, generation and world that we live in. Sin has distorted our view and experience of this, but God's intention and plan will never change.

During the times that I struggled with my self worth and self-esteem, I didn't realise that my struggle was precisely the problem. *Self*-esteem and *self* worth are still rooted in *my* own ability and strength to be a type of woman and prove something to others and myself. It hadn't occurred to me that God was the One who had intimately created me to be a woman, and thus had a plan and a purpose for my life. I didn't realise that I was uniquely and beautifully made to accomplish a purpose that He alone had designed for me, because my eyes were fixed on someone else's worldly standard of living, and not on my heavenly Father's. May we, like David, desire to set our faces as a flint (Isaiah 50:7) upon our Maker so that we may know Him more and the plans that He has set out for our lives.

According to Ephesians 1:4, God knew us in our spiritual form even before we existed on this earth. True liberation, therefore, does not come from our seeking equality with men or competing with one another as women. True liberation comes in the discovering, affirming, understanding and application of who God has created us to be. Liberation only comes when we have truly and wholly connected with our Maker and are found in Him. Only when we have become loosed from the shackles and constraints of this world and our flesh can we experience true femininity as God intended it.

- **As a result of the Fall, we are born sinners – disconnected from God. God made provision through His son Jesus Christ to redeem us into a loving relationship with Himself. When we accept this gift of salvation by faith, we become His –** *spiritually born again.*

Every human is born in sin, and therefore we all have a sinful nature (Romans 5:12). Through Adam and Eve, the inherent inclinations to sin and disobey God entered the human race, and ever since their rebellion, the natural desire of mankind is not to live a life empowered and enabled by God, but rather by the flesh. Our flesh does not desire God, as Romans 8 tells us, and we only have to look at our natural inclinations to see this. Sin has distorted our worldview, and without God we struggle to understand who we are and our purpose; tragically, we are disconnected from our life source. Sin has not only snatched us from union with our Maker; it has also blinded us to His mighty power and work in our lives.

When Adam and Eve sinned, they lost their intimate relationship with God, and this severing caused a spiritual death and disconnect, which would be passed on to all who came after them. We are sinners not because we *do* sinful things; rather, we sin because we *are* sinners. It is a natural inclination, and given the choice to do God's will or our own,

WHO YOU REALLY ARE

we will naturally choose to do ours. This is what makes the Gospel message incredibly powerful – because in our spiritually dead state, God seeks to redeem us and to give us spiritual life anew (Romans 5:8).

To be born again means to be born of God – to be born of the Spirit. God does not desire that we die eternally separated from Him due to sin, and we cannot remove our sins by doing many good deeds or reciting many prayers. His provision for saving us is Jesus Christ, who died on the cross for mankind (John 1:29). After His death, Jesus Christ rose from the grave on the third day to prove that He holds the power over sin and death, and those who have believed in Him are transformed to live a new life, and will also reign with Him eternally (Romans 6).

In recognising our sinful state, we must come to the Lord in repentance, turning completely from our old lives and believing and trusting God at His Word, that Jesus is the resurrection and the life, the only One who can save us from sin and total separation from God. Jesus Christ is the central person in the Gospel, and a woman who has truly encountered Him loses the overwhelming desire to know anything or anyone else so deeply in all the earth.

- **In Christ, we become a new creation and enter into the family of God.**

Sometimes we can find it difficult to believe that we belong to God, because in our physical reality it can be hard to see the evidence of this new spiritual life. Jesus Christ starts the transforming work within our hearts, because this is the very place that needs to be surrendered to Him. The new creation life means letting go of the former way in order to embrace the new way of living with Jesus – no matter what that looks like.

The Bible says in 2 Corinthians 5:17:

Therefore, if anyone is in Christ, he is a new creation; old things have passed away; behold, all things have become new.

This new life is a transformed one, and one of the key signs in knowing that we have been redeemed is our new attitude towards sin. The Holy Spirit helps us to develop new desires, and old habits and desires lose their power and influence over us.

One of the attributes that marks our changed life is our desire to bear good, spiritual fruit unto God.

But the fruit of the Spirit is love, joy, peace, longsuffering, kindness, goodness, faithfulness, gentleness, self-control. Against such there is no Law.

- GALATIANS 5:22-23

When we spend time delighting in the Lord, we can be sure that we will bear good fruit in the right season (Psalm 1:1-3).

We can wrestle at times with not *feeling* as though we are set apart to God because the struggle with unhealthy habits is very strong and can take some time to overcome. The most powerful strongholds over us are in the mind and the heart, and they present themselves in many instances as the things that we have cultivated, practiced and ingrained into our lives – some consciously, others subconsciously, over the years. That is why the Bible encourages us to keep our hearts with diligence (Proverbs 4:23), because all actions flow from this epicentre.

When we live with earthly priorities so magnified in our

view, we will often find ourselves in a place where we are overfeeding our carnal appetites at the expense of our spiritual life. *Have you ever been there?* This inevitably causes spiritual dryness.

In Matthew 16:24, we receive a very specific directive:

Then Jesus said to His disciples, if anyone desires to come after Me, let him deny himself, and take up his cross, and follow Me.

This is the transformed life. Constant, obedient yielding to the Lord's will over ours. This confronts and calls us out of our strong willed and stubborn way to joyfully embrace submission and trust the Lord's guidance and leading of our lives. We can only walk in such a yielded posture when we have a new creation attitude and when our hearts are saturated with love and grace.

- **We have been given a glorious and most privileged mandate of partnering with God to declare this Good News to other women, as well as being the God-led change in our homes, communities, churches and world.**

Receiving such a gift should compel every woman to encourage others to also know God and receive this gift of salvation from Him. Colossians 3:3 tells us that our lives – our *real* lives are hidden in Christ, in God. This means that if we want to find out who we are and what we are here for, we must first look to the Source and Creator of our very lives – God. If we want to understand what our worth and our value are, we must first look to the One who created us to be valuable and considers us to be priceless in His sight.

THE ECHOES OF *YOUR* HEART

- *What do you consider to be the true measure of who you are?*
- *How does being in a relationship with Jesus Christ add significant value and understanding to your life?*
- *How does it feel knowing that you were created to know and walk with God? Does your current lifestyle reflect this?*

A CALL TO ACTION

Take some time to read Psalm 139 and pray, asking the Lord to help you on a new journey of discovering who He created you to be in Him.

THE ECHOES OF HER HEART

WHO YOU REALLY ARE

PART 2
THE ENTRANCE OF SIN

Our identity is rooted in God's created order, and when we deviate from this positioning and truth, we become unhinged, vulnerable and more likely to fall prey to compromise.

4.

THE DISTORTION

I have learned, painfully, that physically attending and participating in Christian activities and events does not always equate to true productivity, and certainly does not prove that a person has a close relationship with Jesus Christ. Although we have many conferences, worship nights, seminars and retreats to encourage us in the faith, it is still very easy to live without the true knowledge and experience of God; desiring everything but the love and lordship of Jesus Christ. It is far easier to be busy *doing for the Lord* than to be *busy abiding in the Lord.*

We live in a time where television and the dominance of the music, social and entertainment industry have become powerful guides that shape our aspirations and life goals. Many young girls are becoming more experimental and promiscuous at a younger age, desiring to grow up quickly – not for more responsibility, but for freedom and autonomy from those that they believe are hindering them from living their *best* lives. There is such a mark of rebellion within us. From where does this desire for such a freedom come?

In order to understand where this desire comes from, we must begin by turning to the pages of Scripture, specifically to Genesis 3, in order to look at God's intent and biblical directives for the first woman who ever lived. In this passage, we will take a look at how the fall of the man and the woman introduced sin into the world and its implication for us as women today. Our identity is rooted in God's created order, and when we deviate from this positioning and truth, we become unhinged, vulnerable and more likely to fall prey to compromise.

The Genesis 3 account is set in the Garden of Eden, which was a place untainted by sin. Everything God made was described as *good,* and there existed a perfect balance of peace, unity, harmony and order between the man, woman and God. Later in the narrative, we see that sin entered the world through Eve, the wife who was given to Adam as a divinely appointed helper. The moment Eve succumbed to temptation and bit into the fruit, of which the Lord forbade her and Adam, and the moment her husband also bit into the fruit, the consequences of their rebellious actions introduced sin into the world, instantly destroying what once was a state of total bliss.

In a flash, both the man and the woman had irrevocably changed the course of humanity's history, and every human born since has been born into sin, with a heart that wrestles between two tensions:

1. Joyfully submitting to God's will for their lives, *or*
2. Choosing to live a self-governing life without God.

The state of the unsaved woman is heart-breaking to God because she is disconnected from Him in spiritual death, and lives only according to the dictates of her earthly appetites.

Many mentions of sin in the Bible are referred to as death.

- ***Physical death:*** Because we are born into sin and live in a sinful body, we die physically and when we do, our spirit and soul will be separated from our physical bodies.
- ***Spiritual death:*** Sin separates us from an intimate relationship with God, disconnecting us from Him. If we remain unsaved at physical death, sin will separate us from God eternally.

Ultimately, sin is separation from God. Without a personal acknowledgment of this and acceptance of redemption through the means of Christ's atoning sacrifice, we cannot live a life unto Him, let alone one that pleases God.

Only when a woman embraces Christ and seeks to willingly come under His covering will she slowly experience the freedom that has been given to her to grow and flourish as He intended her to.

5.

THE FALL

I have a serious weakness for crisps. Although I know that they aren't the best thing to eat, it doesn't curb the inordinate appetite that I have for them. In fact, the more I restrict my access to them, the more my appetite increases, and I'll go to great lengths just to have a salty crunch! There is just something within me that wants what I should not have, and to understand why we possess such an appetite for things that we know are not good for us, we have to go back to the beginning.

When we look at the Genesis 3 account, we notice something quite striking happening within Eve as the serpent accosted her. We see that even though she spoke to the serpent about *not* eating the forbidden fruit, her heart was slowly *yielding* towards doing the exact opposite. Eve *knew* what she had been instructed *not to do* when encouraged to sin against God.

> *Now the serpent was more cunning than any beast of the field which the* LORD *God had made. And he said to the woman, "Has God indeed said, 'You shall not eat of every tree of the garden'?"*
>
> *And the woman said to the serpent, "We may eat the fruit of the trees of the garden; but of the fruit of the tree which is in the midst of the garden, God has said, 'You shall not eat it, nor shall you touch it, lest you die.'"*

- GENESIS 3:1-3

Although Eve repeated God's instructions to Satan, the seed of deception had been sown, and the presentation of an alternative reality suddenly became too irresistible to pass up. This seed sown unfortunately took root in her heart and resulted in a curious and rebellious desire to want to be all-knowing and all-wise like God. She submitted not only to the will of the tempter, but also to her own tainted will and conscience. Eve had already disobeyed God within her own heart before she *physically* ate of the fruit. This is a powerful demonstration and lesson to us. Before a sinful action is manifested, it makes its presence known *within our hearts*, and if we choose to obey, it can pull us away from God and have disastrous consequences that not only affect us directly, but also those who come after us.

There is much to be gleaned in this passage and some of us may be able to relate to this narrative because we have experienced it in our own lives. It is very easy to fall into the trap of having a *form* of godliness – parroting words, reciting scripture and phrases that are recognised and accepted in our Christian circles. We are very familiar with the nuances that characterise Christian speech and appearance; however, Eve's experience is a lesson to us to err on the side of caution, for if the words that we memorise and repeat do not really penetrate our hearts, turning us to God and away from ourselves, we may find ourselves in an uncomfortable and unstable position, contemplating taking a bite out of seemingly attractive, yet dangerous and unbiblical propositions.

> *Then the serpent said to the woman, "You will not surely die. For God knows that in the day you eat of it your eyes will be opened, and you will be like God, knowing good and*

evil."

So, when the woman saw that the tree was good for food, that it was pleasant to the eyes, and a tree desirable to make one wise, she took of its fruit and ate. She also gave to her husband with her, and he ate. Then the eyes of both of them were opened, and they knew that they were naked; and they sewed fig leaves together and made themselves coverings.

- GENESIS 3:4-7

When I read this passage, I instantly thought: *Eve, what about all of the blessings that you had access to because you were the crown of all creation – a chosen, crafted masterpiece of God? You were created to have dominion, to enjoy and co-rule over the earth. Surely you couldn't forget all of that for a piece of fruit?*

Well, she did.

Many expositors have asserted different reasons for Eve being the one who was lured to take a bite of the apple, and we may never fully comprehend what actually happened in this account.

What we do see is that in one moment, Eve had forgotten all of God's instructions and blessings to her, and at the serpent's leading, she focused on what she felt God was withholding from her. Satan planted doubt in her mind about God's character and intention, as well as hitting a nerve that affects us all – *our human desires and pleasures.*

It was the woman who was *first* deceived and tricked into disobedience, and she offered the fruit to her husband, who was with her at the time, and he too ate of it. In that moment, whether they realised the full ramifications of their actions or not, their relationship with God and each other had been impaired.

Since that moment, there has been a disastrous shift in the heart of the woman. Curses were pronounced upon Eve in the areas of childbearing and her relationship with her husband (Genesis 3:16), and we see the effects of this today in our own experience of striving and misunderstanding. Thousands of years have seen generation after generation of women walk upon the face of this earth, and the story remains the same. Now here we are, living in the 21st Century, having lost our sacred relationship with God, and developed commonality with the world. God's order has been tragically violated and reversed.

Love for the world and what it offers has become the norm and too irresistible to ignore. However, this is the very thing that we are encouraged not to love, as 1 John exhorts:

Do not love the world or the things in the world. If anyone loves the world, the love of the Father is not in him. For all that is in the world—the lust of the flesh, the lust of the eyes, and the pride of life – is not of the Father but is of the world. And the world is passing away, and the lust of it; but he who does the will of God abides forever.

- 1 JOHN 2:15-16

In the Genesis 3 account, we see that Eve was lured by the lust of the flesh, the lust of the eyes, and the pride of life – all which led to her downfall. Her desires became distorted and usurped her affection for her Creator.

An even more tragic consequence of the fall is the distortion of God's created order, which begins internally within our very own hearts. When a woman falls from grace, one aspect of her that is deeply marred is her tender vulnerability and beauty that invites and encourages life to those around her. She becomes a dominating, aggressive and controlling woman; a desolate, needy, mousy woman; or a combination of both.

The entrance of sin not only disintegrated the relationship between the man and woman, but between them and God. What has replaced harmony and order is now rebellion, distortion and a striving to *prove ourselves* in this world. This marks the heart of every woman and many of us struggle with the theology of submission because there is a deeply ingrained resistance to it, or a self-sufficient attitude that lies within us. If you look closely at your own life, does this mirror in any way how you relate to God?

Only when a woman embraces Christ and seeks to willingly come under His covering will she slowly experience the freedom that has been given to her to grow and flourish as He intended her to. In our day and age, the agenda to distort, reverse and confuse gender roles and functions is so dominant that you'd have to be living under a rock to not notice or be affected by it!

Only when we begin to seek after and adopt a biblical perspective for male and female roles will we be alerted to our sinful ways and desires, and only when we begin to seek after who we are in Christ and willingly surrender our sin-sick heart to Him, will the veil which separates us from God be removed for Him to enter into the inner chambers of our heart to produce change.

Nevertheless, when one turns to the Lord, the veil is taken away.

- 2 CORINTHIANS 3:16

May we desire and ask the Lord to occupy every chamber of our hearts, for Him to find freedom within us, that He would be truly ours, and we His.

THE ECHOES OF *YOUR* HEART

Eve's experience is a powerful reminder to us:

- She *could have* refused to take the fruit, choosing to be led by truth and not her feelings. *What are some of the ways that we can learn from her experience in our everyday lives?*
- She *could have* treasured the Word of her God and fiercely guarded against anything that would have marred her fellowship with Him. *How can we guard our hearts against prevailing messages that encourage us to seek self-governance rather than God's directives to us?*
- She *could have* resisted the temporary sweetness of sin and embraced the pleasures that endure forevermore (Psalm 16:11). *Are there any areas of your life where you have easily given in to something that temporarily feels good?*
- She *could have* answered the serpent, "Yes! God did really say!" *How can you resolve to be bolder in the Truth of the Word, and present it as a standard against the enemy and his ways?*
- *Can you identify some areas where your understanding of womanhood has been distorted because of messages in the world?*

A CALL TO ACTION

We can resolve to be women who strive to live out what God's Word says to us in our everyday lives, despite our feelings. When we seek to obey God and His ways, we place our trust in Him and can be confident that He will not put us to shame or withhold any good thing from us.

PART 3
A MATTER OF THE HEART

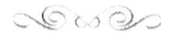

O Holy Spirit, descend plentifully into my heart. Enlighten the dark corners of this neglected dwelling and scatter there Thy cheerful beams.

–Augustine

6.
THE DESIRE OF THE HEART

As a teen, I lived in my own mental and emotional bondage of a Disney-like character whose *beauty was not known – couldn't be known because of the oppression of those around who just didn't understand her*; thus, she lived a less-than-average life, *waiting* for the day when she would finally be found by her Prince Charming, and her life would be forever changed.

I would often sit cross-legged, perched by my small bedroom window overlooking the world, and ask my heart, *Am I beautiful? Am I worth seeking after? Will my day of celebration ever come?* I suppose (if we assume for a brief moment that this folktale was true) that, like Cinderella, a part of me eagerly awaited my Prince Charming's rescue. My rare beauty would blow the world away when that day came, and I would be at peace, knowing that I had *finally been seen.*

I believe that, as women, we all want to be seen in a rare way, and I am no exception. I didn't realise that while I waited for this, I was disqualifying myself from the present. *How would I reach my expected end without the process? When would that day actually come? Today? Tomorrow? Next week? Next year, maybe?* If it never came, would that make my existence and experience on earth any less significant?

The pursuit of our identity, beauty, sense of significance and value is without question still the most sought-after and misunderstood of all feminine desires. Women all over the world ache over these very issues. We may not all be screaming from the rooftops about it, but you and I both know that the desire for enduring beauty, value and worth is there. It may be a loud desire for some and quieter for others, but it is unmistakably invasive.

We ache to know and believe that we hold some type of beauty and are important to those around us. At least once in her life, a woman may ask or think to herself: *How significant am I to the wider world? What contribution does my presence make to others? Am I truly seen?*

We have an overbearing desire – almost a burden and urge for others to notice and appreciate our importance, and some of us need others to see how precious we are even if we cannot fully see it for ourselves. *Can you relate to any of this? Deep down within your own heart, do you perceive this and feel the ache?*

Much of what we see manifesting on the outward finds its roots inwardly. I like to people-watch, and as I watch other women, I often ask myself, *I wonder what's going on in her heart?*

For millions of women *including myself*, we can become worried about the natural aging process because in an ever-moving, fast-paced culture, we are constantly told that although we are pretty today, we will not be tomorrow - unless we take action now. For those who rely on their looks, this can lock them into a quest of trying to maintain their appearance for as long as gravity and time will permit them. There may be some who, in accepting that their outward beauty will not last, wonder if they will be truly content with this and have enough spiritual fortitude and inner depth of character to be comfortable and satisfied with their portion.

We may also recognise deep within ourselves that we have been given the gift and longing to bring forth beauty into this world. We want to be inspirational and a motivating force that no one can deny. We long to unveil our innermost parts to a worthy person and live a life that is rich and fulfilling to us. We long to play a significant role in life – to be the gorgeous, brave, bold, courageous, gentle and feminine image and example of what a woman is, so that the world will know that we existed. Dare I say we have a longing within us that reaches out to grasp the immortal?

It is a human desire; no matter the gender or religious persuasion, we all want to contribute to the world in a significant and meaningful way. Many desire to leave an indelible footprint upon this earth as evidence of them having touched and moved here in their own unique way. You don't have to be a born-again Christian to desire this. Even non-Christians realise this, chase after it and accomplish it in very creative and powerful ways.

Although we are stained with mishaps, misfortunes, sin, struggles and weaknesses, we may sense deep within that part of our identity is linked to the unveiling of a mystery within us – a mystery to talk about and share our story with those who may be able to relate.

Dear lady, this mystery and this beauty are matters of the heart and cannot be uncovered by looking at a fallen world. This beauty, identity, and worth cannot be truly unravelled and displayed through the standards of the world, and it certainly cannot be conjured up by looking *within,* as many popular ideologies suggest.

The type of worth that we seek after can only be affirmed in God. When we turn to Him first, we are faced with the overwhelming reality of our brokenness and are able to recognise our total need for Him to provide the answers to our searching hearts. Do you now see where we have sometimes gone astray? The perpetual sensing, feeling and knowing

within our hearts must lead us to ask: *Lord, help me to understand and know who I am,*
   In You.

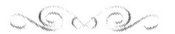

Jesus is the owner of the garden of our hearts, and we have been given the responsibility of stewarding and tending to this garden well.

7.

THE FUNCTION OF THE HEART

Keep your heart with all diligence, for out of it spring the issues of life.

–*Proverbs 4:23*

The heart is a powerful muscular organ containing four main chambers which all work together to consistently pump blood through the circulatory system, supplying oxygen and nutrients into our human body, and removing carbon dioxide and other waste from it. Weighing between 8-10 ounces in women, the heart is vital for the survival of the human body and is important for its physical function.

The movement of the heart itself within the human body is mesmerising; with its many valves, vessels and molecules all contracting and working together to produce its pumping action. Since time immemorial, scientists and doctors have been fascinated with the movement and function of the human heart, for in its very design, it exhibits something incredibly marvellous about God's handiwork. It is simply extraordinary in its ability to sustain the human body.

The heart plays an extremely significant and powerful role when we begin to look at its influence through spiritual lenses. In his book, *The Heart,* James Peto describes the heart as such:

The heart has been portrayed in an astounding variety of ways over the millennia. It is one of our favourite metaphors, and as such, has appeared in stories, poems, religious writings, song lyrics, paintings and sculpture, as a fruit, a flower, a seed bed, a treasure chest, a pincushion, a charm, a fountain, a house, a pump, a pine cone, a wheel, a book.

It flies, it sinks, it grows, it faints, it bleeds, it flutters, it burns, it sings, it rejoices, it breaks, it fibrillates, it stops, it fails. It has an eye. It is attacked, transplanted, sacrificed, wounded, broken, thrown into the sea, given away, written on, occupied, stolen, hidden, swept, polished, eaten, filled, even circumcised.

THE HEART THROUGH SPIRITUAL LENSES

The heart is regarded as the true seat of power, and the core driving force of an individual's thoughts, emotions and decisions. As women, we generally tend to be inclined toward a more emotional state, making it even more vital for us to understand our heart and its effect on our spiritual lives.

Many people believe the mind to be the true determining factor of the decisions that we make in life. In positioning the mind so highly, we can overlook the power and hold that the heart has on us. The mind does play an equally significant role in our processing, justifying and decision-making; however, it is not the only driving factor. You may believe that all your actions, decisions and conversations stem from what you are thinking, but the reality is that what comes out of you, whether by mouth or deed, is a direct result of what is stored within the spiritual chamber of your very own heart. We are wisely advised:

keep your heart with all diligence, for out of it spring the issues of life.

- PROVERBS 4:23

Why are we given such counsel? It is because our hearts are the core of who we truly are. The Matthew Henry Commentary mentions:

We must keep a watchful eye and a strict hand upon all the motions of our inward man. A great duty required by the Laws of wisdom, and in order to our getting and preserving wisdom: Keep thy heart with all diligence. God, who gave us these souls, gave us a strict charge with them: Man, woman, keep thy heart; take heed to thy spirit – Deuteronomy 4:9. We must maintain a holy jealousy of ourselves and set a strict guard, accordingly, upon all the avenues of the soul; keep our hearts from doing hurt and getting hurt, from being defiled by sin and disturbed by trouble; keep them as our jewel, as our vineyard; keep a conscience void of offence; keep out bad thoughts; keep up good thoughts; and keep affections upon right objects and in due bounds. Keep them with all keepings (so the word is); there are many ways of keeping things – by care, by strength, by calling in help, and we must use them all in keeping our hearts; and all little enough, so deceitful are they, Jeremiah 17:9. Or above all keepings; we must keep our hearts with more care and diligence than we keep anything else.

A good reason given for this care, because out of it are the issues of life. Out of a heart well-kept will flow living issues, good products, to the glory of God and the edification of others. Or, in general, all the actions of the life flow from the heart, and therefore keeping that is making the tree good and healing the springs. Our lives will be regular or irregular, comfortable or uncomfortable, according as our hearts are kept or neglected.

During our courting season, my (now) husband and I planned a day trip to Kew Gardens in Richmond-upon-Thames. I was completely blown away by the beauty there. Across 326 acres of land is pretty much every species of plant and flower that you could think of. One minute you're walking through a field of roses and the next, an enchanted jungle. There are secret hidden paths to find and various levels at which you could view the garden. It's beautiful!

This is how I like to think of the heart – as a large garden, and within its confines, different plots representing its chambers. *Imagine this garden* – an epicentre for life or death, depending on how well it is kept. In the springtime, the sun kisses the garden with its golden glow, and buds begin to appear all around, not only adding an array of wonderful colours to its landscape, but to bear witness to the incredible life that this garden brings. A tree casts its shade, giving rest to those who sit under its leaves, and the grass almost sings in unison with the softly blowing wind. All who enter experience peace, tranquillity and beauty.

A variety of flowers fill the air with fragrance, and the melodic sound of birds chirping is a delight to the ear. In the autumn, all leaves shed from the trees, in preparation for hibernation during the winter season, and the ground is enveloped in a sea of golden-brown leaves. When winter arrives, the garden turns into an iced sugar-frosted scene to be admired.

There is often a gate or point of entry into any garden

which requires a gatekeeper to watch over, to prevent animals and unwanted visitors from ruining what lies within it. This *particular* garden is precious, and as such, needs to be tended to. There are specific instructions given to help with the growing of certain plants and the uprooting of grown weeds. In order for the garden to flourish, its grounds must be prepared accordingly so that the soil is ready to receive the nutrients that the gardener will feed it.

Jesus is the owner of the garden of our hearts, and we have been given the responsibility of stewarding and tending to this garden well. Things will need to be pruned, plucked, cut away, uprooted and planted. Wisdom and knowledge are required to sow particular seeds in order to receive the right harvest in the right season.

Sowing.

Once something has been sown into the soil of our hearts, it is programmed there. We store it, our conscience interprets and records it, and then attempts to create a habit out of it; our willpower then actions it, and this is what our lives are built upon – the continuous repetition of the habits stored within our hearts.

How does this affect us spiritually? We have been born into a broken, sin-sick world and taught various systems and ways of living. Before we are awakened and drawn by grace to accept Jesus Christ as our Lord and Saviour, we are thrust into a culture that builds a secular worldview and instils societal expectations and ways in us. This in turn affects and contributes to our foundational expectations, processes and perceptions – all of which come together to form a picture through which we watch, interpret and interact with the world that we live in and the people with whom we live.

Although women are made in the image and likeness of God and are created for His pleasure, in our earthly life there is an aspect of our womanhood that is woven from the very threads of the society, family and culture that we grow up in. In many ways, we are a product of our environment.

In the spiritual realm, the function and purpose of the heart is to love and worship God out of a state of total self-abandonment. However, we can struggle to abandon our lives when we prize our human ways and cultural traditions above cultivating an intimate relationship with Jesus Christ. Without thinking too deeply or thoroughly, we are more likely to notice and more willing to accept the things that fit comfortably into the familiar image of what our earthly lives are supposed to look like.

Have you ever found yourself struggling to accept or live out biblical directives because they are so countercultural to what society has taught us is *normal*? For example, we are all encouraged to store up our riches and possessions in a way that either creates more riches or protects them. Of course, we would all agree that it is wise to establish earthly security and stability. However, the Bible challenges this view with a very outrageous suggestion that even as we work, save and use money, we must in fact maintain a very loose grip in our hearts on money and material possessions:

Do not lay up for yourselves treasures on earth, where moth and rust destroy and where thieves break in and steal; but lay up for yourselves treasures in heaven, where neither moth nor rust destroys and where thieves do not break in and steal. For where your treasure is, there your heart will be also

- MATTHEW 6:19-20

We are also emboldened through advertising and the media to *live our best life now*. We are encouraged to so treasure our lives here on earth that we begin to feel such a sense of personal ownership over the way *we* want to live. We are anxious when we cannot provide adequately for ourselves and when things do not appear as we had envisioned – or as was fed to us. However, here is what the Bible says about us making provision for ourselves:

Therefore, I say to you, do not worry about your life, what you will eat or what you will drink; nor about your body, what you will put on. Is not life more than food, and the body more than clothing?

- MATTHEW 6:25

Within these two passages in Matthew, we are compassionately challenged and urged to lay aside the things that can encumber our hearts so that we can be free to trust in the Lord's provision and care over our lives. This does not mean that we can't enjoy them, but they just must not become the main priority in our lives. Our main priority in life is our relationship with God, and every chamber of our heart was created with the intention of being reserved for this life-giving and life-sustaining union.

This is a powerful reminder – or discovery for some – that everything we build or acquire on this earth is temporary in comparison to eternity with the Lord. Our preoccupation and confidence mustn't be rooted in the things that are transient and fleeting. God gives us the opportunity to experience and enjoy the things pertaining to earthly living; however, He warns us to guard our hearts against the *love and obsession* of these things. We mustn't become so entangled with earthly riches and pursuits that we naively build our identities upon them and measure our success in life by them. Many, in abandoning the Lord to do so, have pierced themselves with many griefs (1 Timothy 6:10). Our hearts must be reserved only for the Lover and Redeemer of our souls.

Our true treasure must be Jesus Christ, and our prayer must be, *Lord, help me to reach a place where I desire and yearn for You more than clothes, more than shoes, more than handbags, houses, my children, my spouse, a car and other things that pertain to this earth. Father, let my heart find rest and assurance in You rather than the false security this world offers. May You remain my portion and always satisfy my deepest needs. Amen.*

I hope that by beginning to look at the spiritual function of your own heart, you are beginning to see just how much you need Jesus to be Lord over it! If we are ever going to have a hope of seeing Him work in our lives, we must totally surrender this seat of power to Him, because it is in this very place that He wants to assert His Lordship.

In our natural state, we cannot desire God nor live in a way that pleases Him. We cannot die to our own self-centred desires and needs when we are not in subjection to God's own will through love. When we come to Christ and we accept and invite Him to be Lord and Saviour over our lives, what we are in effect saying is, *Lord, I am ready for heart surgery. Renew a right spirit within me. By Your grace, do a work within me so that I can live completely for You.*

THE ECHOES OF *YOUR* HEART

- In both the Old Testament and the New Testament, the word *heart* is used to refer to the whole of the innermost part of a person, not merely the emotions. *Have you seen your own heart from this angle before?*
- *Have you given your heart over to anything that has begun to rule over you? What has become your preoccupation and treasure in life?* (Matthew 6:19-20).
- *Have you been challenged to look beyond the physical, to perceive what God is doing within your own heart?*

A CALL TO ACTION

Once something has been sown into the soil of our hearts, it is programmed there. We store it, our conscience records it and attempts to create a habit out of it. Our willpower then actions it, and this is what our lives are built upon – the continuous repetition of the habits stored within our hearts.

- Can you identify any unhealthy habits in your life? Make a list of some of the areas in your heart that haven't been given over to the Lord, and ask Him to help you to surrender them at His feet.

When a woman surrenders her life to God unreservedly, she effectively grants Him permission to enter her world and pour His love, grace and strength into her.

8.

THE PURPOSE OF THE HEART

God, the relationship initiator

God wills that we should push on into His presence and live our whole life there. This is to be known to us in conscious experience. It is more than a doctrine to be held; it is a life to be enjoyed every moment of every day.

-A. W. Tozer – The Pursuit of God

The day I realised that Disney had lied to me when it came to relationships was truly shocking and heart-breaking.

So, you mean to tell me that my handsome Prince Charming is not literally going to be riding in on a horse to sweep me off my feet and declare his unconditional and devoted love for me to the whole world? He isn't perfect? My happy ever after doesn't consist of me being totally head over heels in love every single day with a tall, dark and handsome man? Really?!

When reality hit, I was gobsmacked. You see, like many young girls, I too had grown up having my tender and searching heart guided towards this fantasy that even though there were some scary things out there in the world, my heart would always find its safety and comfort in my saving grace and *one true love* – a man.

I gave the weighty task of keeping my heart to someone

who was just as fallen, weak and fragile as I, and encountered many confusing experiences because I just didn't understand what the purpose of my heart was.

So, what did Disney teach me?

- Disney taught me that love was to be lived out through the emotions.
- That my man would provide my *happily ever after* without ever hurting me, because my heart didn't deserve that.
- Disney taught me that total perfection existed in a man and that as long as I had one, I would be happy for the rest of my life.
- That my chief pursuit in life was to find or be found by a handsome young man and to live in bliss for the rest of my life.
- Love was something that felt good all the time and would mostly always be showered upon me by a man.
- That one day I would be *seen* by the man of my dreams and my life would be transformed. Until then, my current single state of living didn't quite cut it.
- Every girl should dream that a man's kiss will be the key to waking her from an endless slumber, or a dull life.

Now, while most Disney story lines are very endearing, sweet and have a great moral tale to tell; the projection of a damsel who is rescued by the man of her dreams invariably finds itself at the center of the story line. Migrating on from these Disney movies, we then move onto sitcoms and TV shows that further endorse this distortion. Something that seems so innocuous and charming for a young girl to be exposed to, actually sets her up to live with a very distorted and unrealistic view of life and male/female relationships.

So, what is the purpose of our hearts?

We were created to have a relationship with God, and there is no other relationship that a woman will find as fulfilling as the one that she has with her Lord. How wonderful is it then to know that He is the One who initiates that very relationship with us and longs to be our Father, Lover, Friend, Healer, Protector, Provider and All in All.

For the woman, there is truly no one else who can renew, refresh, heal, teach and lead her heart and mind. Her Lord is the only One who can provide validity to all her pursuits in life. Her chief desire, therefore, must be to know Him and to learn to walk with Him daily.

How beautiful and humbling it is to know that the Lord's love for us is not predicated upon our outward performance or appearance, and that we cannot earn it through pious works. It is a divine love. As we grow in our understanding of His pure, holy and endless love for us, we find a rare jewel indeed, for in His love, there is security and the freedom to be all that He has called us to be.

A woman's life is marked by many distinguishing factors: who she says she is, who she thinks she is, whose she thinks she is and who others tell her she is. These components come together to become determinants of how she lives her life, and the value and worth she ascribes to herself. Alongside all of this, she has the joy of navigating through the very real landscapes of her emerging and awakening womanhood in a large world.

It goes without saying then, that knowing who we are is *crucial* to our personal and spiritual development. How can we know the purpose of our heart if we do not look first to its

Creator? We were created and *intricately knit together* for the purpose of fellowship with God through Jesus Christ, and until we find our roots and complete sufficiency in Him, we will be forever searching and making vain attempts to be fulfilled by material things and people who simply cannot satisfy our deep longings.

Our hearts are hungry to be filled, and when we are not spiritually awakened to or stirred toward the Christ life that we have been set apart to live, we are often in a hurry to feed our hearts with void-fillers. Void-fillers are ultimately false structures – people and things that we put into the empty places of our hearts, hoping that in their temporary positioning, they will provide long-lasting fulfilment.

When a woman senses deep within herself a longing for something other than this world and she has not fully awakened to the truth of her identity in Jesus Christ, she can fall into the dangerous trap of freely and easily giving her heart away to an object or person that offers her very *real* yet *fleeting satisfaction.*

So, what then is the true purpose of our hearts, but to exercise the incredible gift and ability to know and walk with God and to fellowship deeply and intimately with Him? This is the friendship, relationship, harmony, comradeship, passion, love and unity that has been restored to us through Jesus Christ.

God created us – men and women alike – so that He could fill us with Himself, help us to experience Him, know Him and live for Him here on earth and in eternity. The heart is like an incubator, and when we are in a true relationship with Jesus Christ, the intention is that we store His Word in our hearts (Psalm 119:11) and apply this Word to our lives through obedient fruit bearing and Christ-centred living. This is good, and brings God great glory.

Many of us have unfortunately grown up not understanding this, and have not been given sound counsel when it comes to knowing the purpose and place of the very real longings within our hearts. Failing to see who Jesus is to us – or not knowing Him at all – causes many women to stumble and fumble their way through the mysterious and complex terrain of life with no biblical blueprint in hand.

May we never lose sight of the fact that we were created to be in *covenant union* with God. This relationship suggests intimacy, communication and love. He created you and me to experience His love and to love others just as He has loved us. As He made His ways made known to Moses (Psalm 103:7), so He desires to make His ways known to you and me. He desires for us to be attuned to His voice as we would to a lover's, to walk with Him as we would with our closest friend and to find covering and guidance under His Headship as we would in a father and husband. All of these earthly relationships and experiences are but a mirror or shadow pointing to the real, life-nourishing relationship that is to be found in God alone.

The woman who does not believe and understand that she was indeed made for God will mistakenly believe that she was made for earthly things, and so hand over her life to those very things. The real purpose for which we were created transcends this world. There is so much more to you than a pair of nice shoes or a handbag. Those things are not bad in and of themselves, but God wants us to enjoy them for what they are and to be mindful that we do not short-change ourselves by placing our identity in them.

As God has initiated this wonderful relationship with us, our task is to wholeheartedly accept it, trust His leadership and press deeply into this most holy and sacred union. We must give our whole lives to it. Once we take that step toward trusting Him to hold our hands and hearts, we will find that He is the only One who can provide the remedy for our ache, quench our thirsty hearts and is the Living Water for all of our parched places.

If you have been on an endless search for fulfilment, and have poured all your heart and energy into a variety of pursuits only to come to the realisation that there is still a deep ache within you, may I suggest that you humbly come before the feet of your loving Father and ask that He help you to draw from His limitless well of grace, mercy and love. His arms are well able, and His counsel is to be depended on. He won't fail you, and He is the culmination of all that you are searching for.

Many of us may find ourselves guilty of having reduced our experience of God to weekly visits to a building called a 'church', to the routines of liturgical sacraments that we perform such as communion or to the many church activities that we participate in. He is so much more to us than these things.

He lives within us and defines the very essence of our lives (Colossians 1:17). Though He cannot be physically seen, a woman who understands the spiritual relationship to which He has called her does not need to see Him in order to believe in Him. She perceives within her spirit that Jesus Christ is who He says He is, because she has received a revelation of Him. This causes her to live out her days on earth courageously and humbly, through the position of faith. Her steps are ordered by faith, and her heart's rhythm is established by her faith in Christ. She can have such a heart posture because she knows the One to whom she is tethered.

For those who proclaim Christ as Lord over their lives, it is important to not only seek *information* on doctrine and living religiously, but to seek a living, dynamic and vibrant *relationship* with Christ, who is at the centre of the Christian faith. Without Jesus Christ filling our everyday lives, it is easy to subscribe to many groups and institutions with the hope of finding meaning. In the end, what we may find is that outside of all the good activity, we are spiritually malnourished, and in our quiet moments, we still do not really know Christ personally. Guilty of this? *I know I am.*

There are many who attend busy church services and functions week after week, yet fail to become impregnated with the potent seed of Jesus Christ Himself, because His life isn't flowing within them. Once His seed is in you, it begins to produce new life from within. So, I encourage you, beautiful lady, to spend your energy and time wisely getting to know this God who has called you into a relationship with Himself. This is also an encouragement and word to myself, as the temptation to fritter my time away with idleness is ever-present. He must become a necessity.

I am urged toward the call to reach through the veil of activity, culture and noise and into the sacred Holy of Holies to touch the very epicentre of it all. God is not far from us. He hears us, is waiting on us and desires us. He, therefore, must become the object of our passionate, intense pursuit. When we walk with Him, we will find that He becomes the foundation upon which our lives are built. He also becomes the underground well that keeps the soil of our hearts constantly watered, nourished and fertile so we can bear seasonal fruit.

When we live intensely with the King of Kings, we can stand boldly in faith against the challenges we face. When we find Christ to be the lover of our souls, we are rich indeed, not with material wealth, but with the confidence of walking with the Creator of the universe. Such a woman does not fear tomorrow because she knows that her Lord is already there, and because He is already there, she is secure in His provision and sustenance. Moreover, she knows where to direct the yearnings of her heart in times of distress, need and joy. She may walk alone, live alone or work alone, but she knows deep within that she is not alone. Her relationship with her Lord invigorates her, carries her and provides her with the hope that she needs to continue pressing in toward Him. What a rich woman she is indeed!

A CALL TO WORSHIP

When you said, "Seek my face", my heart said to You, "Your face, Lord, I will seek".

- PSALM 27:8

There I was, standing in a huge auditorium with 3,000 other women who all professed to love God. I couldn't believe how many faces and voices were present! Over the next few days, some of these women who were strangers would become my friends. When the music slowly rumbled in to signal the beginning of the program, as though on cue, thousands of voices were carried up in unified, harmonious song.

It was dramatic, electrifying and incredibly moving. The atmosphere felt full, and there wasn't an inch of space left for thought of the outside world. When Scripture was read aloud and solos were sung, I would close my eyes to soak in the words and be transported to another place. I sensed community, belonging, sisterhood… and it was beautiful.

During the course of the conference weekend, however, something started to shift slightly within me. As much as I enjoyed the worship services, I suddenly noticed and became distracted by the rehearsed routines. What started off as amazement began to feel a little different. I soon became a little ruffled by all the *things* that were going on in front of me. The multi-coloured lights, thick, smoke screen effects, cinematography, energetic dancers in costumes and bright digital videos had almost become too *loud* for a heart that was earnestly and quietly seeking to have a true encounter with God.

What I desired most was to lay down before the Lord in total abandon of everything, yet I found myself outwardly moving with the swaying of the crowd and responding to the loud music while inwardly asking, *Am I worshiping? Is this what worship is?* I could just sense that what God was drawing me to in those moments was something more temperate, warm and deeper. Something that would require me to go beyond my physical senses of taste, sight, touch, smell and sound to meet with Him spiritually. I first needed to understand what true spiritual worship was from an inward reality. As much as worship is seen in outward expression, its roots lie buried in a heart that is thoroughly surrendered to the Lordship of Jesus.

To worship is to assign value or worth to something or someone. When you worship something, it means you treasure that thing or person above all others, and you make a conscious decision to give that thing or person priority over all other things. Our hearts grow deeper into God the more we offer up ourselves to Him in worship. *Have you taken the time and effort required to offer God your heart of worship?*

Essentially, worship is the language of love, and everybody worships something or someone. You don't have to be a Christian to be a worshipper. The question to ask is: *What or whom am I worshiping?* All of creation was created to display God's craftsmanship, and man was created to fellowship with and worship Him. That was God's original intent – that mankind would live in a posture of unending gratitude, relationship and thanksgiving to Him. If we cast our minds back to the Genesis account, it is clear to see the undiluted and abiding intimacy that existed between God, Adam and Eve before the Fall.

Since the Fall, the inclination to worship still resides within us. It just does not naturally lean towards God. We are no longer completely enthralled by our Maker, as we find that the attention of our hearts is divided among many things. Many of us have traded in God's magnificent glory for worthless and temporary things, as Romans 1:23 says:

... and changed the glory of the incorruptible God into an image made like corruptible man—and birds and four-footed animals and creeping things.

Have you traded in eternal assurance and security for temporary satisfaction and gratification? Worship to Jesus Christ must be an intentional and willing choice that we make within our hearts to God. Every day, God gives us a choice, and He watches to see what we will do with our free will – whether we will choose the fleeting over the enduring. The very act of worship is not found in the songs, dancing and prayers that we offer to God because those acts can be performed even when our hearts are empty and void of an understanding and revelation of Him. Worship first begins within one's own heart before it becomes a lifestyle.

The roots of our hearts have grown into things, and we dare not pull up one rootlet lest we die. Things have become necessary to us, a development never originally intended. God's gifts now take the place of God, and the whole course of nature is upset by the monstrous substitution.

The above quote, from A.W Tozer's book *Pursuit of God*, mentions that *the roots of our hearts have grown into things*. I have found this statement to be so true and timely for the age that we are living in. Our lives are just so full of *stuff*. Too many shoes, clothes, perfumes, etc. – and if we don't have many things, we are in a constant state of pining after them. The problem isn't with the clothing – wanting to look good and presentable isn't a crime. Rather, Scripture teaches us that the problem is our roots. *Where do we draw our sense of identity, worth, value and significance from? What do we worship?*

I tell you, this one had me looking at the floor with a guilty-blank face. I've been there, and in some moments, I am still there – spending hours trying to figure out my sense of style on Pinterest, fashion blogs and YouTube, and then attempting to find all the items that will help me achieve my perfect look. *Things have become necessary to us.* There is such a preoccupation with things in our world, and material possessions and physical comfort have become so important to us.

We often place our worship of objects and people under the guise of *being inspired by someone or something*; however, if we realised just how deeply rooted our idolatry is, it would cause us to pause and reflect. What and who we worship is a big revealer of the posture and inclination of our hearts. *Who or what do you worship? Who gets priority in your life?* Have a look at what David said in Psalm 132:3-5:

> *Surely I will not go into the chamber of my house, or go up to the comfort of my bed; I will not give sleep to my eyes or slumber to my eyelids, until I find a place for the Lord. A dwelling place for the Mighty One of Jacob.*

Here, we see how David willingly chose God, and because of His love for the Lord, he purposed in himself to build a house for Him to dwell in. His love for God compelled him into action – to serve and please Him no matter the personal cost. Does this sound a little bit too intense? This is because it truly is! Worship is deep-rooted because it calls upon you. It requires all your heart, mind, body, soul and *life.* The intensity of this call can make some of us buckle a little when we consider the personal cost. For others, the thought of fully leaning into God can be a fearful prospect, which then causes unfaithful behaviour towards God.

Although we may not say it, we may certainly think: *It requires too much of me.* I have uttered and thought this myself, and still find myself wrestling with truly giving my all to Christ at times. I have come to understand, however, that the highest object of worship that a woman can offer God is herself.

We are worth more than worldly possessions, so when we give ourselves to God, we are giving Him the most valuable thing in all the earth. The words that we use to exalt God in praise and worship, known as *the fruit of our lips*, display the overflow of our heart's adoration toward God. However, did you know that it is possible to offer our money, time, energy, works and words to God without offering our hearts?

Therefore the Lord said: "Inasmuch as these people draw near with their mouths and honour Me with their lips, but have removed their hearts far from Me, and their fear toward Me is taught by the commandment of men.

- ISAIAH 29:13

Ultimately, God desires our hearts. If we praise God

outwardly with our lips and our words as a matter of rote, we have missed the whole point of the relationship that He has called us to. If you have a spouse, your service to him does not flow out of a pretentious heart, but rather, out of a heart filled and overflowing with love. This is how we must live for our heavenly King.

"Now, therefore," says the LORD, "Turn to Me with all your heart, with fasting, with weeping, and with mourning." So rend your heart, and not your garments; Return to the LORD your God, for He is gracious and merciful, slow to anger, and of great kindness; and He relents from doing harm.

- JOEL 2:12-13

There is a temptation for us to become so preoccupied with outward works and service. This can act as a cover for hearts, which have not received a touch or awakening from the Holy Spirit. Before anything manifests outwardly, it must first be exercised in our hearts because what will outward expressions of worship and prayer avail if the inward posture of the heart is not inclined toward God?

The Lord requires our response to Him to go beyond the surface. Rending of the heart is what He desires:

...a broken and contrite heart, which He will not despise.

- PSALM 51:17

I have grown up in 'church', and know how quickly and easily it is to become accustomed to what the *routines* are. I have known *of* God without being *in relationship* with Him, and my Sundays have consisted of getting dressed up to go and sit in a hall full of people listening attentively while I was bored out of my mind!

Worship doesn't begin outwardly, but is the yielding of the whole believer to the fullness of God. It is absolute dependence on *our part* to Christ's total sufficiency. This leads on to further intimacy with God and empowerment from the Holy Spirit. When it comes to worship, we are to *be* the offering required. Our lives must be placed upon the altar, so that the burning of our sinful flesh will rise as a sweet-smelling fragrance unto the Lord.

When a woman surrenders her life to God unreservedly, she effectively grants Him permission to enter her world and pour His love, grace and strength into her. In all His infinite wisdom, knowledge and power, He deposits Himself into her soul; filling her, and imparting spirit-sustaining life into her. *How incredible is that?* This life that our heavenly Father offers can revive the weary heart, mend the broken heart and provide clarity and confirmation to the searching and yearning heart.

Do you see how important our hearts are when we look at this area of worship? It affects and permeates every aspect of our Christian life. When we come to the Lord as new believers, He is the One who creates the clean heart within us, *but we must permit Him to*. To come to Christ with our hearts concealed prevents us from experiencing the intimacy for which we were created. We short-change ourselves in many ways and stunt our own spiritual growth. That is why we need a completely new heart.

Paul implores us to earnestly explore this:

That you put off, concerning your former conduct, the old man which grows corrupt according to the deceitful lusts, and be renewed in the spirit of your mind, and that you put on the new man which was created according to God, in true righteousness and holiness.

- EPHESIANS 4:22-24

Following hard after Jesus Christ is the heart's natural response when it has been captured and is deeply in love with Him. God wants to live this life together with you and I, to share and lead in our days and decisions, our desires and disappointments. He wants intimacy with us amid the busyness and mundane, the meetings, the laundry and long to-do lists. He wants to pour His love into your heart. He wants your deep heart – that central place within that is the truest you.

Moreover, He is interested in intimacy with the woman you currently are, so that He can be the one who causes the growth within you. *Will you enter into this new life of worship with Him?*

THE ECHOES OF *YOUR* HEART

- *Looking at the spiritual aspect of your heart, do you think you guard and cultivate this garden of your heart well?*
- *Are there any other ways that it could be further cultivated?*
- *Are there some things that you worship above God?* If so, list them, and write down *why*.
- *What are the ways in which God is drawing you to Himself?*

A CALL TO ACTION

- Make a list of all the areas that are important for making any earthly relationship work, and parallel that to your relationship with God.
- Ask the Lord in prayer to show you the things that currently pull you further away from Him and relinquish them at His feet.

Pray, asking the Lord to help you to make Him the joy and treasure of your heart. Submit your struggles to Him and request a heart that desires to be rooted and anchored in Him.

Outward adornment has its place, but when weighed against the inexhaustible nature of eternity and our inner personhood, it is fleeting.

9.
A CAPTIVATING BEAUTY

A life spent seeking temporal beauty attains its end, but the life spent seeking the Lord attains imperishable beauty.

***

I possessed a type of beauty that I forcibly and superficially constructed;
blinded to the truth that it was elusive
and I never truly owned it or believed it.
The knowledge of Your love, Lord, has set me free, and in being
awakened to YOU, I now know a
different type of love and beauty.
One that transcends what I see, that is rooted and springs forth from the spiritual to find itself in beautiful bursts and fragrances in the physical. It exudes elegance and is clothed in much grace.
I could think of 100 ways and reasons to denounce this beauty on my worst days, but I cannot deny it because my soul KNOWS it. I am beautiful quite frankly because you say so, and in YOU I have been created to be so.

[EXCERPT TAKEN FROM MY JOURNAL]

***

I could feel an intense heat rising from the soles of my feet to my face. My hands grew clammy as I nervously picked at my red nail varnish. It felt as though someone had placed several fan heaters around me, and I would soon turn into a pool of water right there on my seat.

What am I doing here?

Fidgeting left me in increasingly uncomfortable and in an awkward position.

Just be confident – wait, are my sweat patches visible? Oh gosh, I must have a sweat brow going on right now. What a sight I must be!

As I sat across from confident-looking models at a casting, I couldn't help but feel as though I was an imposter. Yet, ever since I was a little girl, I had wanted to model and emulate the beautiful women who graced the covers of magazines, brand campaigns and our televisions. *The world is theirs, and I want a part of it too.* Their beauty was so rare and irresistible that it opened so many doors in life for them.

I thought about my supermodel idol, Naomi Campbell, as though by thinking alone I would somehow morph into her.

When I grow up, I want to be just like her.

She is a tall, dark-skinned woman who has reached the successful height of supermodel status, and let's not forget to mention, she's absolutely drop-dead gorgeous. It was because of her success that I decided to venture into the world of modelling.

Fuelled with nothing but a big, exciting dream and what I hoped were acceptable looks, I began my journey with such hope and anticipation. It didn't take long, however, to realise that achieving this dream would be much harder than I had thought.

The competition was fierce - because to my surprise, other women also had the exact same dream.

So here I was in this room. You could pierce the atmosphere with a knife, and my efforts at feeling and looking confident were quickly failing me.

I felt sick.

As pretty as I may have looked, no one knew about the extra baggage that I had carried into the room. I was plagued with a heart that was desperate for validation and full of uncertainty and fear – all in pursuit of those most elusive words: *you are most beautiful.*

I didn't get the job, and I spent the next few months writing introductory letters to agencies and trying to arrange face-to-face meetings. After constantly hearing, "You're not quite what we are looking for," I was slowly sinking into the upsetting reality that I would never achieve my dream. I became overwhelmed with rejection because I wasn't pretty enough; or just *enough,* period.

Have you ever experienced that? The feeling of not being enough?

Rejection and I became best friends, and after a while I became so exasperated with my search for a beauty that seemed so temporary, elusive and based upon someone else's subjective view of life. I drew closer to the Word of God for clarity and understanding.

Beauty is a captivating attribute that originates in God, not in our man-made ideas or imagination. As women, we are created and given to the world, just like Eve was, to bring a beautiful, purposeful and God-glorifying strength to our environment. Unfortunately, some of us may have experienced something very different. As we are born into sin, we find that in our attempt to attribute value and meaning to ourselves, we sometimes introduce a *striving*, sharp-edged, dominating and *insecure* energy to our environment. *So how can we possess a captivating beauty?*

"Do not let your adornment be merely outward—arranging the hair, wearing gold, or putting on fine apparel— rather let it be the hidden person of the heart, with the incorruptible beauty of a gentle and quiet spirit, which is very precious in the sight of God"

- 1 PETER 3:3-4

Have you considered how much time you invest in your outward appearance? If you were to lose your looks today, how would that make you feel? Would there be anything left of you? In all honesty, these are tough questions for me to answer, because external beauty does matter somewhat to me. The true beauty defined in the passage above takes a lot of cultivation and inward work, and we cannot discuss aspects of a woman's heart without looking at this topic of beauty.

It isn't a secret that men and women alike desire to be beautiful, and for years have employed several means to preserve or improve their youthful looks for as long as possible. The beauty industry has thrived and continues to benefit from loyal consumers who purchase a variety of products in the pursuit of achieving lasting outward beauty. Every time I walk into a health and beauty retail store, I feel a sense of overwhelm at the amount of variety available! With numerous makeup, hair and skin products in our stores, the average 21st Century woman may be able to attest to having tried a plethora of products in her own attempt at discovering what works best for her and compliments her the most.

While it is important to take care of our outward appearance, it is even more important to desire and cultivate the inward beauty that radiates from us as a result of our relationship with Jesus Christ. Gaining this type of beauty requires a painful, yet necessary process of exposing and stripping of the old self and its desires, and giving our hearts to God for Him to fill us from within.

When I read 1 Peter 3:3-4, it struck a chord with me because the writer addresses something that is so important for us women to grasp. True beauty transcends culture and outward features. True captivating beauty disregards whether you have good skin or not, how long/short, straight/curly your hair is; it is so much more than how curvaceous or slim you are, whether you have a large bust or not, and it certainly transcends the clothing you wear.

God created women to be beautiful and to reflect His beauty, so we will always have that desire to be beautiful. There is something captivating about a woman taking care of her appearance and dressing up. With that being said, our pursuits and desires should not centre wholly upon our outward adornment. The One who can make us feel truly, irrevocably beautiful is God, but just like misplaced identity, we can find ourselves being misled when it comes to the issue of beauty. We can erroneously believe that we will be more beautiful if we could only *enhance this, lift this and tuck that.*

The Word of God admonishes us to turn away from the obsessive attention of outward things to focus on Him, because when we do, we edge closer to His goal for our lives, which is *holiness.* The simple fact is that outward beauty does not last. Everything eventually wears away, and there will always be something or someone more beautiful and in vogue. Outward adornment has its place, but when weighed against the inexhaustible nature of eternity and our inner personhood, it is fleeting.

Adornment is defined as:

Something that adds attractiveness; ornament; accessory. Ornamentation; embellishment.

Think about it: When it comes to outward beauty, there is often an intentional choice made to put something on in order to look a particular way. It must be the same when it comes to cultivating inner beauty, because focusing on our character is far more important. We are not captivatingly beautiful until we radiate and are a reflection of Jesus Christ. When God looks at us, He does not judge by external factors, but rather our heart's posture. So to others we may look well groomed, but if our hearts are not right before the Lord, we do not bring pleasure to our heavenly Father.

A woman is captivatingly beautiful when walking in meekness and submission to God; she places the claims, pursuits and life of Christ before her own. A woman whose life is inclined to and totally surrendered to Christ develops a character that is rooted in Him and overflows from Him. May we be women who reflect the Father's heart – who are beautifully broken in spirit and who say with such boldness, *Less of me, Father, and more of you.*

THE ECHOES OF *YOUR* HEART

- *What is your definition of beauty?*
- *What is God's definition of beauty?*
- *When it comes to enduring beauty, what can you learn from 1 Peter 3:3-4?*

A CALL TO ACTION

God created women to be beautiful and to reflect His beauty, so we will always have that desire to be beautiful. There is something captivating about a woman taking care of her appearance and dressing up. With that being said, our pursuits and desires should not centre wholly upon our outward adornment.

- Why do you think inner beauty is regarded as more important than outward beauty?
- Can you identify some ways that you could begin to cultivate lasting inner beauty?

THE ECHOES OF HER HEART

PART 4
BROKENNESS

In the next few chapters, we will explore a broken heart from the following perspectives:

1. The sacredness found in heartache
2. The sacredness that can be found in abandonment
3. The strange fruit of brokenness
4. A surrendered heart - beautifully broken

In allowing His healing to take place in our hearts, we learn something profound about love. True love does not have conditions. It loves in spite of, not because of.

10.

A SACRED PAIN

He heals the brokenhearted and binds up their wounds.

-Psalm 147:3

Fear not, for I am with you; be not dismayed, for I am your God; I will strengthen you, I will help you, I will uphold you with my righteous right hand.

-Isaiah 41:10

I remember my first heartbreak. I was in secondary school, and a boy that I liked embarrassed me in front of all of our peers. I recall going home that afternoon feeling *physical* pain. I had been utterly rejected and cried, but after the tears, I felt a strong sense of sorrow at the thought of someone being so cruel. *I mean,* this was just because of a teenage boy! It sounds silly thinking back on it, but at the time, my heart was experiencing and processing something new that I would go on to experience in different ways later on in life.

We have all experienced heartache in one form or another, and in this chapter, we'll look at how we can take the heartache, rejection, betrayal and abandonment, and bring them to the feet of a very loving and involved Father who really does care about our afflictions, and every single one of our needs. It is important to first emphasise that even in the moments when it does not feel like it, we can choose to see the sacred in our difficult moments by connecting with the truth that there is a lesson in them for us, and that God identifies with our heartache. He is not far removed from our problems, so even when it feels as though we cannot sense or see His fingerprints in our toughest moments, we must remember that we do not walk through painful seasons alone.

The Lord is fully locked in and engaged with every detail of our lives, and longs for us to experience the true depth and magnitude of His love toward us. In order to do this, we must look at heartache from a new vantage point - that of God's perspective, before we address our own. We must begin with God because if anyone can relate and talk about heartache, it is He.

Firstly, in creating mankind to have free will, God introduced the opportunity for us to willingly choose Him, rather than demanding robotic obedience. In doing so, He not only created the opportunity for a wonderful loving relationship with us, but also, He opened His heart up to the risk of profound heartache, which we see so vividly in His (Old Testament) relationship with mankind after the Fall. God has walked the road of heartache and abandonment Himself.

The children of Israel are often cited for their rebellious, ignorant and ungrateful attitudes and responses to God's continual demonstration of love, protection, provision and affection. Time after time, God did whatever it took to win their attention and affections, and The Old Testament recounts the way the Israelites ignored this, flaunting their love for other gods and man-made objects whilst God's grace and mercy was available to them. Since the beginning of time, God has known what it feels like to live with a broken and hurting heart caused by a rebellious people who did not respond in thankfulness and love to Him.

Then the Lord saw that the wickedness of man was great in the earth, and that every intent of the thoughts of his heart was only evil continually. And the Lord was sorry that He had made man on the earth, and He was grieved in His heart.

- GENESIS 6:5-6

If we take the journey right back to Genesis 3, we see that Adam and Eve had a great opportunity to walk in closeness with God, yet they rejected the relationship He offered in exchange for a hollow promise from a crafty serpent. Ever since time began, we humans have been breaking God's heart; yet His love for us remains the same. The prophet Jeremiah recounts the way God aches over our rejection of His love for us in husbandry language. Speaking of the people of Israel, He said:

My covenant which they broke, though I was a husband to them.

- JEREMIAH 31:32

At one point in time, we have grieved God's heart in our dismissal of Him for others, and in our human weakness, we continue to do this. If anyone has endured the heartache that comes with abandonment and betrayal, it is God. Bringing this topic closer to us, let's think about the emotion that typically accompanies our broken hearts. Anger? Frustration? Regret? experience pain, we automatically resort to negative associations and actions due to the blinding intensity of the hurt. Rarely does one consider heartache to be sacred.

When it comes to pain, we have two choices:
1. We can choose to see heartache as an opportunity to draw nearer to the Lord for His comfort.
2. We can choose to allow ourselves to become overwhelmed and overcome by the feeling of heartache and pain.

The woman truly seeking spiritual maturity leans into the pain she feels as she determines to identify more with her Lord in His pain. Her heart, though it may not fully comprehend, understands that the cultivation of maturity does not only occur in the pleasantries of life. In some mysterious way, then, when our hearts are broken by those that we love and have trusted, we should seek to lean into this maturing process, seeing it as a new opportunity to draw closer to the very experience and character of God. We have an opportunity to glean divine wisdom and be humbled even in the midst of our own agony and disappointment.

Therefore, the challenge to us as women on a journey of refinement and sanctification is to search for His lessons within the pain and ask, *Lord, what are you seeking to teach me from this experience?*

David the psalmist and King of Israel was described as a man after God's own heart and is one example of a person who walked closely with God during the most testing and trying seasons of his life. Through the trials, moments of fear and truly crushing times, his love and yearning for God remained constant, and it even intensified.

The righteous cry out, and the LORD hears, and delivers them out of all their troubles. The LORD is near to those who have a broken heart, and saves such as have a contrite spirit. Many are the afflictions of the righteous, but the LORD *delivers him out of them all. He guards all his bones; Not one of them is broken.*

- PSALM 34:17-20

But I will sing of Your power; Yes, I will sing aloud of Your mercy in the morning; For You have been my defense and refuge in the day of my trouble.

- PSALM 59:16

Pain can make us feel crushed. We may shed many tears and feel alone, or abandoned. Pain can so discourage us that it alters the state of our hearts. We can grow to become despondent, resentful and bitter when our expectations of people are not met. But did you know that with every painful experience that we go through, we are given the opportunity to deepen our capacity of loving without conditions, as well as experience God's healing? Heartache presents us with incredible access to growth.

The healing process may take some time, and at times it can be excruciating, but with it comes growth, which is necessary for our wholeness. God is the Great Physician who can bind up our broken pieces and put them back together, but He can only do this when we give these fragments to Him.

In allowing His healing to take place in our hearts, we learn something profound about love. True love does not have conditions. It loves in spite of, not because of. Many of us have grown up with a distorted view of love, and our understanding is that A must add up to B before love can flow. But true love is not restricted by equations and expectations. True love flows *despite* the equation. Can you love someone, forgive him or her and see him or her as God sees them regardless of how they behave? This is a true, Christ-centred love.

Heartache in the form of betrayal is something that most of us may be familiar with, and we must remember that just as God is not a stranger to a broken heart, He is also not a stranger to betrayal. We see this in one of the most incredibly powerful illustrations in scripture, when the prophet Hosea was called to live out an earthly parallel of God's relationship with His people Israel. Upon God's instruction, Hosea married Gomer, a woman who was compulsively unfaithful to him every single chance she was given.

Time after time, she betrayed him, yet he consistently took her back, loving her against all logic. God used the life drawing of Hosea and Gomer to demonstrate just how betrayed He felt over Israel's abandonment of Him. He had taken Israel unto Himself, but when Israel gave her affection to other gods, she threw His love for her back in His face.

Before our broken hearts lead us to resent God, perhaps we could take this time to consider how we, in our misunderstanding, rebellion and resistance have been so unfaithful to the God who has redeemed us unto Himself. *How are we so different today to Israel thousands of years ago?* We flirt with other gods in the form of people and material things, yet God waits patiently to restore us to Himself.

THE ECHOES OF *YOUR* HEART

- *Can you identify the similarities we share today with Israel thousands of years ago?*
- *Can you love someone, forgive them and see them as God sees them regardless of how they behave?*

A CALL TO ACTION

- Bring to the feet of Jesus all those that have hurt you, and ask the Lord to heal your heart and give you the capacity to understand from His point of view and to forgive.

THE ECHOES OF HER HEART

SOME SCRIPTURES TO ENCOURAGE THOSE WITH A BROKEN HEART:

Cast your burden on the Lord, And He shall sustain you; He shall never permit the righteous to be moved.

- PSALM 55:22

...casting all your care upon Him, for He cares for you.

- 1 PETER 5:7

For I consider that the sufferings of this present time are not worthy to be compared with the glory which shall be revealed in us.

- ROMANS 8:18

The Lord is near to those who have a broken heart, And saves such as have a contrite spirit.

- PSALM 34:18

And God will wipe away every tear from their eyes; there shall be no more death, nor sorrow, nor crying. There shall be no more pain, for the former things have passed away.

- REVELATIONS 21:4

My flesh and my heart may fail; But God is the strength of my heart and my portion forever.

- PSALM 73:26

In our abandonment, it can be asserted that we are uniquely and divinely poised in that very moment to intimately experience something that God Himself has experienced.

11.

SACRED ABANDONMENT

No matter what storm you face, you need to know that God loves you. He has not abandoned you.

-Franklin Graham

Nobody likes to feel abandoned. It isn't a pleasant experience for anyone to go through, yet so many of us do experience this feeling every day. Just like a broken heart, we hold negative associations with abandonment because it hits a painful nerve within us and communicates to us that we are unworthy of another's friendship and attention. When we find ourselves having been abandoned by someone we love and trust, there is life-giving comfort in knowing that God can identify with this pain and need for companionship, because He has experienced it. We therefore must go to Him with our hurts in the knowledge that He can and does comfort and heal us. There is much beauty and sacredness to be found in abandonment, and we can see this in the life of Jesus Christ.

At the end of Jesus's time on earth, when He was preparing Himself spiritually and emotionally to be handed over as a lamb led to the slaughter, one can only imagine what was going through His mind and heart. Consider the scene in the garden of Gethsemane in John 14:32-50. In what could be described as arguably the darkest hour of Jesus' life, when His *soul was sorrowful, even to death,* He gathered in this garden with trusted friends and disciples to pray and seek spiritual strength for what was about to come upon Him. Jesus asked His disciples to stay with Him, to be watchful and to pray. As He poured out His grief to His Father, they fell asleep due to physical fatigue. When the Roman soldiers approached them, they were not adequately prepared, and due to sheer terror, most of them fled to save themselves from being arrested or killed.

Betrayal and abandonment are written all over this scene. Jesus had spent the last three years with these men and had shared intimate fellowship with them. Yet at this crucial time when He needed them, they betrayed, rejected and denied Him. God Himself knows what it feels like to be abandoned. So, when you find yourself in a place of abandonment and it seems as though your entire world has been turned upside down and your heart is broken beyond repair, remember that nothing about this space is unfamiliar to your Father.

In our abandonment, it can be asserted that we are uniquely and divinely poised in that very moment to intimately experience something that God Himself has experienced. We can take comfort in knowing that God is ultimately the One who holds our very lives together, even when we cannot see or feel His hands. He never abandons us, as Scripture tells us:

When my father and my mother forsake me, Then the LORD *will take care of me.*

- PSALM 27:10

SOME SCRIPTURES TO ENCOURAGE THOSE DEALING WITH HEARTACHE AND ABANDONMENT:

He heals the broken-hearted and binds up their wounds.

- PSALM 147:3

When my father and my mother forsake me, Then the Lord will take care of me.

- PSALM 27:10

For I am persuaded that neither death nor life, nor angels nor principalities nor powers, nor things present nor things to come, nor height nor depth, nor any other created thing, shall be able to separate us from the love of God which is in Christ Jesus our Lord.

- ROMANS 8:38-39

Can a woman forget her nursing child, And not have compassion on the son of her womb? Surely they may forget, Yet I will not forget you. See, I have inscribed you on the palms of My hands; Your walls are continually before Me.

- ISAIAH 49:15-16

Look on my right hand and see, For there is no one who acknowledges me; Refuge has failed me; No one cares for my soul. I cried out to You, O Lord: I said, You are my refuge, My portion in the land of the living.

- PSALM 142:4-5

When we do not know to Whom we belong and the purpose for which we were created, we will always sell ourselves short and cheaply, and it will always begin within the inner chambers of our hearts before it is outwardly manifest.

12.

A STRANGE FRUIT

Whatever failure you and I make of our lives, we do not make because God forces us to do so. In whatever way we go wrong; we do not do so because God planned that we should. We do it because of our own willfulness and wicked rebellion against God.

-Clovis G. Chappell

A broken heart can also lead to rebellious and promiscuous behaviour. Without the holy pursuit of inward wholeness and fulfilment in Jesus Christ, a woman errs in her understanding of where validation and affirmation come from. As a result, she takes her brokenness into various situations and finds herself entangled with different people and things. *Have you ever experienced this in your own life?* I know I have.

We often associate promiscuity with sexual immorality, and rebellion with lawlessness, defiance and delinquency because they are outwardly seen. Rarely do we make the link between these outward expressions and the inward state of our hearts.

In Genesis 3, the Fall of Adam and Eve resulted not only in a deep destruction and breach in the divinely appointed relationship between the man and woman, but also a huge chasm between the whole of mankind and God. At the root of all of our undesirable thoughts and actions lies a fundamental inclination toward rebellion and promiscuity. *We just want to do our own thing.*

Eve's desire since the Fall would not only be inclined to work destructively against her husband, but it would unfortunately tend toward dysfunctional thinking and living, as well as resistance and opposition to the direct authoritative hierarchy and order of her God, *who is her ultimate husband.*

Biblical principles of submission and authority are topics that many modern women tend to feel uncomfortable discussing because of our instinctive repulsion to them. As the *offspring* of Eve, we now have an overbearing desire that does not pull us closer to God, but rather further away from Him, and we have inherited a rebellious desire that craves the world and the gratification of our flesh more than to walk and live in intimacy with God, and under His authoritative rule.

Our hearts are mirrors, reflecting the worldly things that we so love and cling on to, so closeness to God is a position that we must cultivate our hearts to enthusiastically desire.

As women born into sin, without the Holy Spirit transforming our hearts and causing us to yield to Him, our actions and behaviours typically will be displeasing to God as pride, arrogance and rebellion characterise our attitude in life. Consider the puffed-up women of Zion who were judged by the prophet Isaiah for their rebellious ways:

Moreover, the LORD says: Because the daughters of Zion are haughty, And walk with outstretched necks And wanton eyes, Walking and mincing as they go, Making a jingling with their feet, Therefore the Lord will strike with a scab The crown of the head of the daughters of Zion,

A STRANGE FRUIT

And the LORD will uncover their secret parts.

In that day the Lord will take away the finery: The jingling anklets, the scarves, and the crescents; The pendants, the bracelets, and the veils; The headdresses, the leg ornaments, and the headbands; The perfume boxes, the charms, and the rings; The nose jewels, the festal apparel, and the mantles; The outer garments, the purses, and the mirrors; The fine linen, the turbans, and the robes.

And so it shall be: Instead of a sweet smell there will be a stench; Instead of a sash, a rope; Instead of well-set hair, baldness; Instead of a rich robe, a girding of sackcloth; And branding instead of beauty.

- ISAIAH 3:16-24

Isaiah described the women of Zion as haughty. They were disdainfully proud, arrogant, conceited and contemptuous. The behaviour of these women included craning their necks, flirting with their eyes, walking with dainty steps and twinkling their ankle bracelets to gain attention from passers-by. In their brokenness, the women of Zion walked, talked and lived like women with no sense of real value.

These women were not acting as they should have been because they did not know who their Father was, and thus where their true identity lay.

Such has been the case with women in the past, but can you find similarities among women in our modern world? Without a true knowledge of our identity, we make ourselves up to appear a certain way; meanwhile, we are broken and barren within.

The hearts and minds of the daughters of Zion were *filled with Eastern ways*. This was the world and the pagan culture in which they lived – a culture steeped in idol worship and alternative lifestyles that led them to stray away from the Lord. These women had traded in their true God-given value for worldly approval and material objects, and it resulted in undesirable behaviour.

When the purpose of anything is not understood, it is misused and abused. In our own brokenness and separation from God, we lose our sense of worth and purpose. When we do not know to Whom we belong and the purpose for which we were created, we will always sell ourselves short and cheaply, and it will always begin within the inner chambers of our hearts before it is outwardly manifest.

If we become preoccupied with tending to the physical in order to appear a certain way, but fail to adequately tend to our spiritual lives, we risk becoming like the *whitewashed tombs* that Jesus warned about in Matthew 23:27:

"...which indeed appear beautiful outwardly, but inside are full of dead men's bones and all uncleanness."

It does not appear that our culture generally cares much for true inner beauty, and it is no secret that there is a preoccupation with outward looks, with an overwhelming number of celebrities, social media accounts and television shows driving us toward the obsession of prizing outward things over our inward spiritual state.

Cultivating earthly beauty must rank second to cultivating spiritual inner beauty. Some of us know, accept and believe this, yet we can still find ourselves wrestling with the tensions that exist within our hearts. I wonder: Have we become so aware of our bodies and how badly they need a treadmill, and so conscious of our faces, our nails and hair that even with our good intentions, we have gradually allowed ourselves to become spiritually numb?

Complete focus on the outer and neglect of the inward can leave us beautiful on the outside and broken on the inside. In the book of Hosea, Gomer conducted her harlotry in a shamefully flagrant manner. What drove her to this? It's quite clear to see that she was a broken and unrooted woman searching for wholeness; however, the consequences of her actions, especially the agony she caused her husband and children (Hosea 2), were the unavoidable realities of her spiritual barrenness.

In order to fill a deep void within herself, Gomer sought her own enjoyment so irresponsibly that she ultimately wound up in bondage to the very thing that brought her pleasure. But due to his unconditional love for her, Hosea sought after his wife and redeemed Gomer from her shameful state. He paid the price for her and brought her back to himself. He restored her as his wife after an initial period of discipline to help reorient her life to the vows she had made to him in marriage.

What is truly striking in this beautiful yet painful story is that a rebellious woman who was so deep in promiscuity was joined in a covenantal relationship with an upright, God-fearing man. A little like how a dog goes back to its own vomit, Gomer would creep out of her marital home to go and sleep with other men. I am sure she appreciated Hosea's love, but she was bound like a slave to a lifestyle of rebellion and promiscuity, born out of a *sin-sick, broken heart*.

While God used the story of this man and woman to illustrate a profoundly broader truth of Israel's conduct towards Him, I cannot help but relate to the smaller story and think: *Poor Hosea, why couldn't Gomer just love him and stay faithful to him?*

Interesting, or rather, sad, isn't it?

How many of us do this exact same thing with God? Emotionally and spiritually prostituting ourselves to the world because we have had a taste of other things? Although we have been saved and are in a relationship with a wonderful, covenant-keeping God, we still turn our eyes away from Him to bow down to the other gods in our lives. *Oh, I couldn't even begin to count the number of times I too have been like Gomer.*

We may love the Lord, but our lifestyles hold us captive because we have given them so much authority over us. We worship many things, and our hearts have developed an appetite for these things. So, when God is assuring us that we have everything that we will ever need in Him, we can struggle to *really* believe this, and wrestle with its practical outworking in our lives.

You see, whatever we give ourselves over to, we begin to *crave* more of. Becoming a Christian does not mean that all of our appetites instantly vanish. We have acquired particular tastes for dressing a certain way, speaking a certain way and desiring a certain lifestyle, all of which do not necessarily bring glory to the Lord.

In order to fully and personally experience God, to drink deeply and astronomically from His never-ending well, we must ask that He becomes our *complete* delight and that He weans us from the things that we love and instinctively choose above Him.

When we indulge in things that do not sustain the spiritual life in us, we will starve spiritually and grow weak in that area of our lives. Our flesh will grow stronger, and we will yearn to further satisfy the lusts of the flesh.

More often than not, it isn't that we do not desire to grow in our relationship with the Lord. But deep down in our hearts, we don't want to let go of the things that we enjoy in the world. We somehow feel as though we will be short-changing ourselves because, after all, *"It's just fun, it's not harming anyone and it's not sending me to hell."*

It may not send us to hell. However, the greater tragedy would be that we will never have the opportunity to *meet* this Jesus that we claim to follow here on earth, and if we are not cautious, what appears to be just a little fun will blossom into full rebellion and entanglement. Our lives will be fully occupied with *doing, showing, and performing,* when what we truly need is for God to move in a mighty way in our hearts that we may be drawn back into His loving arms and remain there.

THE ECHOES OF *YOUR* HEART

A broken heart can also lead to rebellious and promiscuous behaviour. Without the holy pursuit of inward wholeness and fulfilment in Jesus Christ, a woman errs in her understanding of where validation and affirmation come from. As a result, she takes her brokenness into various situations and finds herself entangled with different people and things.

- *Can you identify in any way with the story of Hosea and Gomer? Have you ever been entangled with something or in rebellion to God?*
- *Do you have a rebellious streak in you concerning your relationship with God? Can you see where this may have come from?*

A CALL TO ACTION

- Come before the Lord, and if necessary, ask for forgiveness if you have rebelled or grieved Him through your behaviour/actions and words.

- Identify ways that the world encourages rebellion towards God, and how you are encouraged to live according to a different standard.

There is no other antidote that can heal a diseased and deceitful heart but Jesus Christ.

13.

A DECEITFUL HEART

The heart is deceitful above all things, and desperately wicked; Who can know it?

– Jeremiah 17:9

The prophet Jeremiah uttered these powerful, sobering and true words concerning the heart, and its abilities. Our heart can deceive us and lead us away from the will of God for our lives. That is why God must have all of it, and not just a part of it. It is important to remember that our natural inclination is not for godly things, and this is why it is so important for us to open our hearts up and willingly permit the Holy Spirit to do an uninterrupted work within us.

The word *deception* is defined as 'the act of propagating beliefs in things that are not true, or not the whole truth (as in half-truths or omissions)'. There is also self-deception, which as it suggests, means an individual deceives himself or herself. Deception tends to occur in romantic and platonic relationships when trust and loyalty have been abused. Self-deception also occurs when we convince ourselves of a piece of information so that we can act (or not act) upon it. Deception has its root in sin, and when a woman is not surrendered to Christ, she is carried along by her deceptive desires that are masked as truth.

As women desiring to mature spiritually and make Jesus Lord over our lives, we must be aware of the power of deception and intentionally pray that we do not become entangled in its web. It is only when we have a true understanding of how we can easily deceive ourselves that we realise our desperate need for the intervening, sustaining grace and mercy of God. As women, we quickly learn how best to present ourselves to others. But getting dressed up and spraying on sweet perfume cannot hide a potent stench: We are desperately sin-sick, and it corrodes us from our deepest being.

We mustn't buy into the false message that we can easily cover up our sin-sick hearts by pretending that sin does not exist, or that it does not hold any power over us. A wise and meek woman brings her heart to her Lord, understanding her many shortfalls, and that only in Him can her mind be constantly renewed, and her heart *charged* toward willing submission and obedience to God. We must lay a new, firm foundation and receive a new heart. From our first birth into this earth, we were born into sin and iniquity, as David so vividly states:

Behold, I was brought forth in iniquity, And in sin my mother conceived me.

- PSALM 51:5

That is why in order for us to be reconciled to God, a new (spiritual) rebirth was needed in order for us to be fashioned and made alive in Jesus Christ. God had to begin from the foundation, doing away with the old so that He could build new bedrock within us – a foundation that would give birth to a new, Christ-empowered nature with renewed principles, affections and purpose. It is important for us to realise the true state that we were in before Christ, and the state we can find ourselves in without Jesus Christ.

We mustn't underestimate the power of deception. If we search deep within, we will see how our lives can be so wedded to the desires of our carnal nature that we become imprisoned to our own human-centred will, seeking to make provision for it every chance we get. What communion can there be between God and a soul in this sin-sick condition? It is like a disease – a corruption that is bred in the bone with us, which leads us on to make decisions that are not God-honouring.

Conducting an honest appraisal of our spiritual condition with and without Christ propels us toward change. Much of our wrestling with God originates from our hearts, and when we are steeped in carnality, we do not have a desire for the things that spiritually convict us, change us and ultimately draw us closer to God. That is why the born-again Christian rejoices so much in Jesus!

It is because of His selfless sacrifice that Christians stand in a privileged position before God. Believers are beckoned to come boldly to His throne of grace (Hebrews 4:16) with their prayers and petitions. He welcomes them with open arms because He has wiped away their transgressions. *Hallelujah!* There is no other antidote that can heal a diseased and deceitful heart but Jesus Christ. No amount of good works can ever eclipse the release of grace and move of the Holy Spirit as He does a reconstructive work in the heart of a woman ruled by deceitfulness.

TRUTH-LED VS. EMOTION-LED

Deceitfulness can also occur when we are led by our subjective emotions and feelings, rather than the objective truth. In the words of Elisabeth Elliot:

Obedience to God is always possible. It is a deadly error to fall into the notion that when feelings are extremely strong we can do nothing but act on them.... Keep a tight rein on our emotions. They may remain, but it is not they who are to rule the action. They have no authority. A life lived in God is not lived on the plane of the feelings, but of the will.

The prevailing and popular message in our culture is for us to live in our feelings, throw caution to the wind and *follow our hearts*. This is an unbiblical concept, yet many of us can find ourselves succumbing to the strong pull of our emotions in our everyday decisions. According to Proverbs 28:26:

He who trusts in his own heart is a fool, but whoever walks wisely will be delivered.

We are often encouraged to listen to our hearts, and in many ways, we have been conditioned to place a high value on our feelings; however, God's desire and directive to us concerning this area of our hearts is a very different message to that of the world.

Feelings change according to outward circumstance and inward appetite, and because our emotions and feelings are rooted in our flesh, they do prove to be unstable. In order to make sober-minded and wise decisions, it is important that we yield our hearts to God and request that He directs our emotions to fall in alignment to His perfect will for our lives.

Surrendering our emotions to the Lord is not always something that we feel inclined to do; however, if He really is Lord over our lives, we must prize His directive for our lives above our feelings of comfort and preference.

THE ECHOES OF *YOUR* HEART

As women desiring to mature spiritually and make Jesus Lord over our lives, we must be aware of the power of deception and intentionally pray that we do not become entangled in its web.

- *Have you ever followed the deceitfulness of your heart, only to realise that it was leading you into a ditch? What did you learn from that experience?*

A CALL TO ACTION

- Ask the Lord to show you the true state of your heart. Write down what He shows you and ask Him to help you surrender its inclinations to Him.

A woman who has totally surrendered her heart to the Lord is a beautifully broken woman, whose desires for earthly achievements and possessions are diminishing due to the opportunity afforded her to know her Saviour intimately.

.

14.

BEAUTIFULLY BROKEN

The sacrifices of God are a broken spirit,
A broken and a contrite heart—
These, O God, You will not despise.

-Psalm 51:17

THE ECHOES OF HER HEART: JOURNAL ENTRY

Reckless abandonment. What does that mean, Lord? I have gone through my entire teenage years and early twenties not being aware of this phrase It didn't mean much to me, until I realised that whether I was aware of it or not, I had partaken in whatever these words implied. Reckless… it reminds me of how I threw myself so easily and hurriedly onto material things and people. I was consumed with others' thoughts of me. I was hungry for their validation. I needed them to give substance to my life and tell me who I was because I didn't know.

Whenever I looked in the mirror, all I saw was someone who always came up short – never quite the pretty girl, the slim girl or the popular girl. I needed to have a title. Frustratingly, I knew that deep down, I didn't even want to have the validation, because I knew that it was masking something more serious in my heart. Yet I still needed to know that somebody in this world thought I was worthy enough to be considered. I suppose then, yes, Lord, I gave myself away. I felt that I had no other choice because I didn't know You, and I didn't know myself.

Although validation from others never lasted long – because it never can – I craved and lusted after it. It was like a drug. It was the food I thought I desperately needed for my malnourished soul. What I did not know, Lord, was that I needed to surrender it all to You. Reckless abandonment is something that is reserved for You alone and no other. In giving it to others and to things, I still remained dry. What was I supposed to do with my heart that was craving love and affection? I was to give it to You and drink hungrily from the well that never runs dry.

[EXCERPT TAKEN FROM MY JOURNAL]

***

Brokenness before God is a result of a true spiritual work that has been performed and is continually at work within our hearts. This kind of brokenness does not necessarily originate from any physical condition or ailment, nor is it a one-time occurrence; but rather, it is a distinctively divine work wrought only by the Holy Spirit deep within our hearts. It takes a woman who has come to the end of herself to be truly awakened and broken over her sin before God. Such brokenness welcomes a true dealing with everything within ourselves that grieves the heart of God and separates us from

Him.

When I reached this state of brokenness in my walk, it felt as though I was having an out of body experience. Standing on the outside looking within, I was overcome by grief because I was finally seeing God with my spiritual eyes. I could see how He was the answer to what my heart had been searching for, and my anchor, and assurance. I suddenly saw where I had been going wrong, and instead of feeling shame, I felt an overwhelming sense of *relief and love.*

I had found my refuge, and I became desperate for repentance and to let the light into all my dark, wayward and wondering places. God in His loving kindness met with me - *at my ugliest.*

It is far too easy to think of repentance as *I am sorry*, while our hearts are still in bondage to the very things that cause a great chasm between us and God. True brokenness goes far beyond this, requiring a walking away from oneself. The Greek word for repentance is *metanoia*, meaning to have a different and new mind than what once was. When a woman is deeply repentant, it is because she recognises her sin and its awfulness in the sight of a holy and pure God.

The Holy Spirit does a marvellous work of placing a mirror before us, causing us to compare our squalid depraved state to that of a pure, perfect Lord. *Who could dare stand before such brilliance without receiving within themselves such a keen awareness of their position, and an eager and ravenous desire to be stripped of all that is displeasing to their Lord?* When we realise where we stand with God, we are compelled toward brokenness and a total emptying of ourselves before Him.

True brokenness describes a state which clothes the heart in *a baptism of anguish and sorrow,* when it considers how far it is away from God. This leads to an overwhelming urge within us to turn away from our sinful ways to allow God to transform our hearts and minds to be patterned after Him.

In true brokenness before Jesus, we will find something most beautiful: a desire, cleaving and yoking to that which is noble, just and pure (Philippians 4:8). Ultimately, it is a deep identification with Christ and death to our own selves.

When I think about a surrendered and beautifully broken heart, I remember the sinful woman who anointed the feet of Jesus with her costly perfume. She demonstrated reckless abandonment to her King, which stands as a challenging encouragement to us. Let's take a look at her story.

JESUS ANOINTED BY A SINFUL WOMAN

Then one of the Pharisees asked Him to eat with him. And He went to the Pharisee's house, and sat down to eat. And behold, a woman in the city who was a sinner, when she knew that Jesus sat at the table in the Pharisee's house, brought an alabaster flask of fragrant oil, and stood at His feet behind Him weeping; and she began to wash His feet with her tears, and wiped them with the hair of her head; and she kissed His feet and anointed them with the fragrant oil. Now when the Pharisee who had invited Him saw this, he spoke to himself, saying, "This Man, if He were a prophet, would know who and what manner of woman this is who is touching Him, for she is a sinner." And Jesus answered and said to him, "Simon, I have something to say to you" So he said, "Teacher, say it."

"There was a certain creditor who had two debtors. One owed five hundred denarii, and the other fifty. And when they had nothing with which to repay, he freely forgave them both. Tell Me, therefore, which of them will love him more?" Simon answered and said, "I suppose

the one whom he forgave more." And He said to him, "You have rightly judged." Then He turned to the woman and said to Simon, "Do you see this woman? I entered your house; you gave Me no water for My feet, but she has washed My feet with her tears and wiped them with the hair of her head. You gave Me no kiss, but this woman has not ceased to kiss My feet since the time I came in. You did not anoint My head with oil, but this woman has anointed My feet with fragrant oil. Therefore I say to you, her sins, which are many, are forgiven, for she loved much. But to whom little is forgiven, the same loves little."

Then He said to her, "Your sins are forgiven." And those who sat at the table with Him began to say to themselves, "Who is this who even forgives sins?" Then He said to the woman, "Your faith has saved you. Go in peace."

- LUKE 7:36-50

Luke refers to this nameless woman as a sinner, and it is mentioned that perhaps she was a prostitute who walked the streets of Nain in southwest Galilee. Seeking to be made whole, this woman desperately approached Jesus one day when He was at the house of a Pharisee. The powerful moment in this story comes when, disregarding those around her, she took a courageous, reckless and faith-filled step toward Jesus with her alabaster box.

Without saying a word, she dropped to her knees and wept at His feet. She then used her hair to wipe the tears that she shed and poured the expensive oil that was in her alabaster box all over His feet, anointing Him in worship and honour. This woman brought all of her shame, her needs and all of herself to Jesus. She was beautifully broken at His feet and Jesus responded to this woman with tender love and great mercy.

She had leaned into Him, and in doing so, emptied herself into Him. In His graceful, loving response, He leaned back into her, filling her with Himself. What would appear to be a physical act of recognition was really much deeper than that. There was spiritual communion between this woman and her Lord.

Her sins had been forgiven. This story tells of a woman who appears to have had enough of what the world offered her. She had turned from all that she had known to come desperately to God with all of her heart, mind and body. Her act is a demonstration of a woman whose heart was totally surrendered to God.

The ointment from her alabaster box that was poured at Jesus's feet was also extremely significant. In ancient times, a young woman or her family purchased an alabaster box for her in preparation for covenantal marriage. This box was a precious item. The size of the alabaster box, and the amount of ointment inside it was directly proportional to the wealth of that family and the value of the woman. This alabaster box would be part of her dowry (the wealth transferred from the bride's family to the groom or his family, ostensibly for the bride).

If a young man pursued a woman, seeking her hand in marriage, she would respond by taking the alabaster box of perfume, which represented her value and worth, and pour it at his feet. This gesture of anointing his feet showed that she recognised and honoured him as her head and covering, and that she was ready to be wed to him – *ready to be his bride.*

Picture this sinful woman pushing her way through the naysayers – her own fears, and the thick cloud of shame standing accusingly before her as she presses on into Jesus.

Her heartbeat.

The hot tears running fast down her cheeks.

Her hair.

Her face lowered close enough to the ground to taste the dirt.

Her trembling body shaking uncontrollably as she edges ever closer to the throne of mercy and grace – the throne of her King. The overpowering smell of the sweet perfume that was poured out, filling the entire room with the aroma and fragrance of humility, surrender, love and redemption. This woman displayed a profound sense of awareness and reverence for Jesus.

She had given everything that she possibly could to the world. Her emotions, her mind and her body had been recklessly tossed around in her hope of finding an anchor for her soul. Yet, nothing had proven to be sufficient, and so she finally relinquished control and came before Jesus, broken. With her actions, she engaged in a deeply intimate, spiritual act of worship to Jesus.

Her actions demonstrated an acknowledgement of God's divine hierarchical order of headship and submission – one that her repentant and humble actions indicated that she was more than willing to conform to. By pouring the perfume at Jesus's feet, she gave Him all of herself: all of her dreams, her passions, fears and everything that would constitute to and identify her as being a woman.

She laid it all at the feet of Jesus in a wonderful act of desperation, submission and adoration. She brought her broken self to His feet because she knew that He could heal her and make her whole.

This account is a great witness and encouragement to us because it is a display of a woman who had *done it all* concerning worldly pursuits, yet that had not been enough. Only Jesus was enough, and that's why she found herself at His feet. Customarily, the ointment from an alabaster box was to be poured at the feet of a man to whom she was to be betrothed, but here, she was pouring it at the feet of Jesus.

What looked to be behaviour considered disdainful by those around her was actually a very moving and private encounter, which Jesus accepted.

This woman shed tears at Jesus's feet and then wiped the tears with her hair. A woman's hair signifies her glory. Through this act, she was surrendering her glory to Jesus. It's wonderful how at that very moment, because of her heart's posture and because she had given Jesus her glory, her shame was instantly removed, and she displayed a Christ-radiating glory. She hadn't been shamed by Jesus, but loved into freedom.

Jesus used her actions in that moment as a good example to the disapproving and condemning Pharisee. He blessed and forgave this woman because of the love she had shown Him, and because of her repentant heart. When we get to a place where what grieves God grieves us, we can finally begin to draw closer to the Lord and permit Him to work through us.

A woman who has totally surrendered her heart to the Lord is a *beautifully broken* woman, whose desires for earthly achievements and possessions are diminishing due to the opportunity afforded her to know her Saviour intimately. Such a woman unreservedly casts all that she is at the feet of Jesus because she has total confidence and faith that He is the only One who can uphold and permanently anchor her life.

Furthermore, this woman realises that all she could ever

hope to be is found in the Creator of her life. Being keenly aware that she is far from perfect, she seeks to *continually* relinquish all that she is to a loving God who is able to do for her far more than she can do for herself. Brokenness is not a call to *self-perfecting behaviour*, but rather an acknowledgement and renunciation of ourselves in order to embrace Jesus ever the more and have Him fill our lives completely.

ABDICATION

This word indicates an act of renunciation of one's own authority and control to oneself or something else. A woman whose heart is in surrender to God understands that she must step down from the throne of control and hand over that position in her heart to her Lord every day. God must take over the driving seat of her heart in order to transform her desires and entire life.

Furthermore, the woman who has surrendered her heart to Jesus has eternity in mind and lives with heaven's view in her sight. Earthly things depreciate in value when compared to living in the will of her Father here on earth. The goal and chief preoccupation of such a woman is to draw near to her Lord in deep spiritual knowledge and personal experience. A woman with this understanding knows that if she tried to save her own life, it would be a completely futile attempt.

> *For whoever desires to save his life will lose it, but whoever loses his life for My sake will find it. For what profit is it to a man if he gains the whole world, and loses his own soul? Or what will a man give in exchange for his soul?*

- MATTHEW 16:25-26

Our willingness to become true disciples of Jesus Christ will cost us significantly. Surrender, as its name suggests, requires us to willingly give up our rights to the most precious part of us – *our hearts* – in recognition that our lives no longer belong to us once we accept Jesus as our Lord. He is more than capable of looking after our lives and using them for His own glory and purpose.

In a world that encourages us to be bosses of our lives, the propagated agenda is to inculcate independence from authority, accountability and order, making ourselves the highest and most authoritative voice over our lives. This message has also trickled into the church. We have bitten into the lie that God places unrealistic and demanding burdens upon those who choose to have faith in Him and follow Him. From this viewpoint, the notion of submitting one's entire life to God is met with offence and much resistance, as life appears to be much more attractive outside of this tyrannical and obsessive dictator's grip. This message is simply not the truth.

What is beautiful about this story of the sinful woman and Jesus is the fact that *she* pressed through the veil of culture to renounce the throne of her heart to its rightful owner. She spoke no words. What was there to say? Jesus knew, and she knew.

Naturally, we wouldn't be able to perform such an act in our own strength, because if truth be told, *it is not within us to turn to God and seek Him with all our hearts*. It is only the stirring and working of the Holy Spirit within us that can kindle warmth, like the heat of a flame, from a cold and darkened heart.

What a beautiful illustration of God's grace.

It is my earnest prayer that we do not grow weary of surrendering and abandoning our hearts to the Lord, but that we may be humble enough to approach the throne of grace daily, with a desire and a delight to pour it all at the feet of the Father.

THE ECHOES OF *YOUR* HEART

- *What are some of the joys and blessings you have experienced as a result of surrendering some things to Jesus?*
- *Are there some parts of your heart that you are shielding from God?*
- *What makes you afraid to surrender?*

A CALL TO ACTION

- Would you be willing to pour out your heart and life to Jesus?
- Perhaps begin to study the heart behind *abdication* and surrender in the context of your relationship with God and ask Him to help you to honour Him in such a way.

BEAUTIFULLY BROKEN

PART 5
AN UNVEILED HEART

We must make it our hearts' desire and mission to know the One who has called us, because without the desire to know Him, we fall prey to the world, growing ever more insensitive to the voice of our Bridegroom.

15.

A SENSITIVE HEART

When You said, "Seek My face,"
My heart said to You, "Your face, LORD, I will seek."

-Psalm 27:8

I lay on my bed and looked straight upwards to the ceiling. I had awoken that morning to a mind filled with what felt like a million thoughts. Adverts I had seen on the television flashed across my view, conversations I had with people played over and over again, along with wonderings of what my day would consist of. How long was my to do list? What demanded my attention right now, and how could I conquer the day *before it had even started?* I desperately wanted to wake up with Jesus on my mind, but found that it was such a struggle. I felt so distracted, and desensitised to the voice of God.

Have you ever felt this way?

In a world saturated with various messages and alternatives, we are hard-pressed with so much information that it is not only exhausting to make choices, but it is also difficult to differentiate and discern truth from deception. Within these murky waters, we must set our sights on becoming women who fight to develop and maintain the ability, discernment and discipline of hearing God through His Word and appropriating this Word to our everyday lives.

Moreover, we must make it our hearts' desire and mission to know the One who has called us, because without the desire to know Him, we fall prey to the world, growing ever more insensitive to the voice of our Bridegroom. Our Beloved is constantly calling us to pull away from the distractions of the world, and there is truly much satisfaction, stability, joy and purpose to be found when our hearts are set upon the true Cornerstone from which all else is built.

God is constantly speaking. The question is: *Are we listening?* We must wrestle with this if we are to ever encounter the freedom and beauty that comes with walking in intimacy with the Lord. It is important to remember that we are created in God's image. God is a spirit, and He created us to commune with Him in spirit. Genesis reveals to us that the first thing that God did after creating Adam was to speak to him. So, if we are in Christ, and He in us, we have the ability to hear God!

As we are created in His image, we are capable of responding to God by His grace. In the midst of our busy days, advertising, millions of daily Christian messages being pumped through social media, as well as the influence of our peers, it can be very difficult to *hear* the voice of the Lord, or to discern and know His direction for our lives personally. We therefore must develop the discipline of being in a posture of waiting before the Lord, as David was:

My soul waits for the Lord. More than those who watch for the morning—Yes, more than those who watch for the morning.

A SENSITIVE HEART

- PSALM 130:6

There are many things that the Lord longs to unveil to us if we would only take a moment to turn our gaze, and quieten our hearts before Him. Developing sensitivity to the Lord does not suddenly happen as though by magic. It requires great consideration, care, effort and attention to lovingly choose Jesus above the noise and worldly alternatives. When we come to Christ, He tells us to leave all that we have known behind us and to be enthralled by His love for us. We can only experience the intensity of His love when we say 'yes' to Jesus, and we keep saying 'yes' to Him every single day.

We must lovingly *cultivate*.

We first come across this word *cultivate* in the Garden of Eden account – Genesis 2, to be specific. It was used in connection with the instruction given by the Lord to Adam to *tend and keep* (Genesis 2:15) the garden that he had been placed in. To cultivate means to foster growth, to refine, tend to and improve. We have been given the opportunity to cultivate all that the Lord gives to us. It goes without saying then, that as He has presented us with the gift of salvation and an opportunity to walk in close relationship with Him, we must desire and create intentional ways of cultivating this relationship, as we would any other significant relationship.

Remember the garden?

In order to maintain sensitivity to His voice, it is important to be attuned to it, or we do not stand a chance in preserving our spiritual passion. What often begins with eagerness and devotedness can very quickly head down a rapid decline, so to combat the tendency to slip into insensitivity, we can cultivate the habits of prayer, Bible study, journaling, meditation on the Word and fellowship with other believers.

God also speaks to us through His Word. As we study and read, the Holy Spirit convicts us and illuminates a new understanding and revelation within our hearts. God can speak through absolutely everything and anyone, and the Holy Spirit will always lead us towards a life that glorifies God.

Biologically speaking, there is a case to be made for the way that women are "wired." There are many unique details within our design which ultimately point back to our Creator. Considering the nature of the woman, it would not be implausible to say that we are moved more by our emotions and a sense of relatedness. We have higher levels of oxytocin (a bonding hormone which makes us nurturing and maternal) in our brains, and this causes us to seek out meaningful relationships and emotionally complex experiences. The female brain, differing to that of a male, has been designed by God to be more sensually oriented. This means that we tend to lean more on and rely on physical and emotionally intimate moments.

We know that since the Fall the unique qualities and designs of both men and women have been severely corrupted, but if we look at them from the perspective of God's intended purpose, we can see something truly unique and beautiful here. Perhaps our composition as women was intended to demonstrate and display a deep, intimate part of God that only a woman can fully experience and exhibit?

It is possible that when God created woman, He created all of her senses, intuitions and emotions to interact on a deeper spiritual level, not only to be a suitable helpmeet for her partner, but also to be able to function and move in a very detailed and intimate way with her Lord.

Biologically as women, we know the power of emotional bonds in ourselves, and how this intensely drives our behaviour in the relationships we have with our loved ones and children. *How much more does this point to the spiritual sphere and our relationship with God?* Perhaps we have lost this insight amidst our pursuit of worldly things; however, this is the place that God desires each one of us to be in Him: the place of intimacy.

THE ECHOES OF *YOUR* HEART

- *Have you noticed yourself being distracted with concerns of the world when you should be focusing on Jesus?*
- Think of some ways that you can cultivate sensitivity to the Lord.

A CALL TO ACTION

- Identify and write down some of the things that distract you and pull you away from being motivated towards living a life with Jesus.
- Ask the Lord to help you eliminate these distractions, so that you can develop a desire for Him.

THE ECHOES OF HER HEART

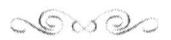

The woman whose heart has been circumcised to the Lord has accepted the call for Christ to govern all of her actions, desires and plans.

16.

A CIRCUMCISED HEART

In Him you were also circumcised with the circumcision made without hands, by putting off the body of the sins of the flesh, by the circumcision of Christ.

-*Colossians 2:11*

To circumcise is to cut. In order to fully experience God and His character, to walk in His will for our lives, and to be used for His glory, we must have our hearts circumcised – cut from the ways of the world, so that we can live set apart to Him. Paul says:

> *but he is a Jew who is one inwardly; and circumcision is that of the heart, in the Spirit, not in the letter; whose praise is not from men but from God.*

- ROMANS 2:29

WHAT DOES CIRCUMCISION REALLY MEAN?

Male circumcision was and still is a practiced rite in many cultures and religions. In the Bible, we first see the act of circumcision in Genesis 17 as the defining covenantal moment between God and Abraham, his household, and every generation that would come after him. This was the beginning of the nation of Israel.

Physical circumcision then, was a mark of this covenant and involved the cutting off the foreskin of a man. This external sign demonstrated that an individual was set apart and devoted to *Yahweh*.

The act of circumcision was so significant that as part of God's instruction, all those who were found to be uncircumcised would be considered to be breaking this covenant, and therefore cut off from His blessings. Since physical circumcision began, those who subscribe to the Abrahamic religions thereafter have practiced it. Paul in Romans 2:29 discusses an Old Testament Law and its application to New Testament believers. Paul asserted that physical circumcision is only of value if one can observe the Law in its entirety – which *of course is impossible for anyone to do!*

To further hammer this point home, Paul boldly stated that since God had introduced a new covenant through Jesus Christ, pleasing Him hinged upon a person's childlike faith in Him. He was hinting at the astounding fact that Jewish circumcision is only an *outward sign* of being set apart to God. Jesus often addressed the importance of the inward posture of the heart, explaining that if the heart's inclination is sinful, then physical circumcision has no value. *A circumcised body and a sinful heart is a paradox.*

With this understanding, rather than depending on outward

rituals, Paul focuses the spotlight on the state of the heart, which is a more consuming endeavour. He uses the act of circumcision as a metaphor to assert that having a pure heart before God is only due to the work of the Holy Spirit in a willing believer. The Holy Spirit causes change in the heart of the believer, and this is what Paul refers to as the *circumcision of the heart*.

God has always sought for a meaningful, living relationship with us. His desire is for us to possess a heart to love, know and follow Him. We see this in Deuteronomy 30:6:

The Lord your God will circumcise your hearts and the hearts of your descendants, so that you may love him with all your heart and with all your soul, and live.

The physical act was pointing to an inward inclination; however, the people of Israel only focused on the outward – the *letter* of the Law, without truly embracing the attitude behind it – the *spiritual* meaning behind the Law. It is so easy for us to focus on God's instruction, rather than the meaning behind His instruction. *Have you ever noticed this in your own life?*

Just as physical circumcision is performed by cutting away the flesh of the foreskin, spiritual circumcision cuts away the fleshly parts of us. Paul's statement in Romans 2:29 refers to having a pure heart, separated unto God. This type of circumcision must reach the heart of every believing woman, cutting away everything that acts as a barrier between her and her God. It is a circumcision that cuts deep into the soul, the essence of who she is, her attitudes and relationship with the world so that she can be truly set apart from the world unto her Lord; not just outwardly, but inwardly. *Circumcision of the heart is a call and acceptance to holiness and consecration to*

Jesus.

The distinguishing mark of those who are not circumcised is that they seek only that which gratifies the flesh. In doing so, they resist the Lordship of Jesus Christ. If our senses, appetites and passions lead us, then we can be likened to the blind, feeling our way through life, subject to our own desires. I myself did not realise that I had unhealthy appetites until God's grace-filled Word began to slowly knead through my own resistant heart.

> *Circumcise yourselves to the LORD, And take away the foreskins of your hearts, You men of Judah and inhabitants of Jerusalem, Lest My fury come forth like fire, And burn so that no one can quench it, Because of the evil of your doings.*
>
> - JEREMIAH 4:4

For us to mature, bear fruit and see the hand of God in our lives, we are encouraged to release all that we are to Him, being open to the fact that He desires to come in to rearrange and change our lives for good. It may take years, or a week for us to be weaned off of certain things. However long it takes, God promises us that He is committed to our sanctification, and that He will never leave us nor forsake us – we need only remain in Him for the work to be done. His Word is permeated with so many beautiful and affirming promises that He is for us, He is at work in us and He will complete all that He has begun within us to the glory of His name.

The woman whose heart has been circumcised to the Lord has accepted the call for Christ to govern all of her actions, desires and plans. A life devoted to faith, not self, is the distinguishing mark upon her life.

THE ECHOES OF *YOUR* HEART

- *Did you know that having a relationship with Jesus means that you are set apart and special to Him?*
- *What is the Holy Spirit showing you that you are set apart from, and set apart for?*

A CALL TO ACTION

Circumcision of the heart is a call and acceptance to holiness.

- Which areas of your life do you sense God calling you to come up higher into Him? Identify them, write them down and ask Him to teach you how.

When we draw away from Him, we soon grow cold and distant, vulnerable to compromise and accommodation to what the world offers.

17.

A RESOLVED HEART

*I have set the LORD always before me;
Because He is at my right hand I shall not be moved.*

-Psalms 16:8

Have you resolved yet? Are you resolved in your heart about the type of woman you want to grow to become in the Lord? Often, we have an idea of what we want to achieve in life and where we want to be at the turn of each year; yet, do we give our spiritual lives as much thought when it comes to resolving to live wholeheartedly for Jesus Christ? There is a big difference between making resolutions and being resolved in your heart about something.

1. To be resolved in anything means that we are settled and have decided firmly on a course of action concerning a specific thing, person or lifestyle.
2. To be resolved speaks of a deep conviction that has transformed us and continues to astonish us daily.
3. To be resolved is to take a stance and to be bold in a declaration that stands true to the life that Jesus Christ has called us to.

Women redeemed by God would do well to make a sure commitment toward their spiritual growth, and to be a beacon of light for the Lord Jesus Christ. God gives us the free will to make choices, and we must use this free will to make an intelligent and willing decision to choose Jesus above everything the world offers us.

You are the light of the world. A city that is set on a hill cannot be hidden. Nor do they light a lamp and put it under a basket, but on a lampstand, and it gives light to all who are in the house. Let your light so shine before men, that they may see your good works and glorify your Father in heaven.

- MATTHEW 5:14-16 (NKJV).

How can we be a bright light shining for Jesus when we have not fully resolved in our hearts to follow Him no matter the circumstance? Being resolved within your heart does not mean that trouble will not arise. It means that no matter what arises, you have decided upon a course of action, which requires constant forward motion, rather than backwards. Being resolute means that you are anchored to something greater than yourself.

Our culture is increasingly becoming more and more diverse, and while this may provide great opportunities for commerce, business, trade, relationships and the like, it also brings with it several opportunities for compromise due to views, opinions and lifestyles that are framed as 'alternative', rather than contradictory to truth. Whether you are a Christian woman who has been on a journey with Christ for quite some time and are seeking to consistently grow, or you are a new believer who is just experiencing Jesus for the first time, you won't be immune to the pull of the culture upon your own heart.

Scripture teaches us that there is only one God. Monotheism is a sound, tested and biblical truth that we must ingest; yet in our fast-moving society, we can find ourselves having many gods in the form of objects and other man-made items.

Committing ourselves to a lifestyle of discipline in the Lord will certainly test us. Therefore, if we do not cultivate the habit of intentionally resolving to keep our hearts and eyes upon the Lord, we will be tossed around by the culture in which we live. We must remember that as disciples of Jesus, though we are in this world, we are not of it (John 17:16); not part of its values, nor representing its systems.

A resolved heart does not make decisions based on emotions, nor is it sustained by them. Such a woman's life is anchored to the truth of God's Word and in desiring to live a life of no compromise, a woman whose heart is resolved has heaven in her sights and upholds the rewards that Scripture affords her. She chooses to love God with all that she is and with everything that she has – *not perfectly,* but certainly humbly and hungrily.

HOW CAN WE CULTIVATE A RESOLVED HEART TOWARD JESUS?

One of the key areas to look at is remaining and abiding in Jesus continually. When we draw away from Him, we soon grow cold and distant, vulnerable to compromise and accommodation to what the world offers. In John 15:1-8, Jesus says:

I am the true vine, and My Father is the vinedresser. Every branch in Me that does not bear fruit He takes away; and every branch that bears fruit He prunes, that it may bear more fruit. You are already clean because of the word, which I have spoken to you. Abide in Me, and I in you. As the branch cannot bear fruit of itself, unless it abides in the vine, neither can you, unless you abide in Me. I am the vine, you are the branches. He who abides in Me, and I in him, bears much fruit; for without Me you can do nothing. If anyone does not abide in Me, he is cast out as a branch and is withered; and they gather them and throw them into the fire, and they are burned. If you abide in Me, and My words abide in you, you will ask what you desire, and it shall be done for you. By this My Father is glorified, that you bear much fruit; so you will be My disciples.

A vine is a plant that has a long, slender stem which trails or creeps on the ground, or climbs upward by winding itself around something. It can be rooted in the soil, but it has most of its leaves in the brighter, exposed area, getting the best of both worlds.

A vinedresser is an agriculturalist involved in the daily pruning and cultivation of grapevines. Vinedressers work nearly year-round to help ensure the vineyard has a successful crop from which to create wine and juices. Vinedressers work diligently to ensure that the vine bears fruit. Jesus Christ is the Vine – the true chosen and promised Vine, our Source and Saviour. To continue to remain nourished, to receive the right nutrients and to bear fruit – to live a life of purpose, to pass tests, to fully emerge into the women that God foreknew before the beginning of this world – we must remain in the Vine, Jesus Christ.

Remaining in Christ is where we must be resolved to be because we cannot bear Christ-like fruit outside of Him. It is only through him and in Him that we can flourish. Our first course of action, therefore, is to decide that we are going to wait before Him and live in fellowship with Him before any other.

THE ECHOES OF *YOUR* HEART

- *What are the things holding you back from resolving to live for God wholeheartedly? What could you do to minimise or eliminate these things?*
- *How will your resolve be different from a New Year's resolution?*

A CALL TO ACTION

Are you resolved in your heart about the type of woman you want to grow to become in the Lord? Often, we have an idea of what we want to achieve in life and where we want to be at the turn of each year; yet, do we give our spiritual lives as much thought when it comes to resolving to live wholeheartedly for Jesus Christ?

- Write a short paragraph about the woman that you desire to be in the Lord and ask the Lord to teach you how to grow into a woman after His heart.
- Place this note in a location where you can see it often, and be encouraged to remain resolved!

THE ECHOES OF HER HEART

Holiness is not a call to perfection, but to single-mindedness, single-heartedness, sincerity and loving intentionality towards God.

18.
A CALL TO HOLINESS

True holiness, we surely ought to remember, does not consist merely of inward sensations and impressions. It is much more than tears, sighs, bodily excitement, a quickened pulse, a passionate feeling of attachment to our favorite preachers and our own religious party and a readiness to quarrel with everyone who does not agree with us. It is something of "the image of Christ" which can be seen and observed by others in our private life, and habits, and character, and doings! (Romans 8:29).

-J.C. Ryle – *Holiness*

Our months tend to be filled with many socials, and if you are anything like me, you may be constantly celebrating the "extraordinary" milestone events in your family and friends lives. From holidays, birthdays, engagements, pregnancy announcements, weddings, new jobs, new houses, cars etc., it can sometimes feel as though we are moving from one social event to the next, congratulating, squealing, hugging and dancing our way through our days. While there is absolutely nothing wrong with this (in fact, they are great ways to foster and strengthen godly friendships and rejoice at the faithfulness of God in others' lives), there is something even more significant about the heart that draws away from all the activity and noise to seek the Lord's face for true relationship, because it understands that as much as we are called to one another, we are first called to our Him, our Maker.

God is holy, and holiness is a characteristic unique to His nature, which we see displayed from Genesis to Revelation. The words holiness and holy occur hundreds of times in the Bible, meaning that it is an important aspect of God that we must take note of. Any woman called to be a disciple of Christ is called and encouraged toward holy living because God is holy.

Just as He chose us in Him before the foundation of the world, that we should be holy and without blame before Him in love.

- EPHESIANS 1:4

WHAT IS HOLINESS?

As with circumcision of the heart, holiness cannot be fully lived out if it first does not originate from the heart. Holiness is an attitude of the heart and reflects a person, place or thing that is sacred and has been divinely consecrated unto God. I'll be the first to admit that at first glance, the word holiness, depending on your experience of church and God, can feel burdensome and like a heavy sack of large stones weighing you down.

In our well-meaning attempt to please God and *do well* in our Christian walk, many of us may have fallen into the trap of trying to overcome feelings of shame and guilt by setting an impossibly pious standard that we ourselves cannot live up to- all in the name of being *holy*. In doing so, we can experience the harsh realities that come with adopting a legalistic approach to the meaning of this word holiness. The context and the right teaching of holiness matters.

Like circumcision, the principle root word for holiness in the Old Testament is to *cut* or to *separate*. This is an indication that holiness means *to be taken out and set apart* from something else – the world and sin. In the Bible, we note that several places, days and people were considered holy. Moses's first encounter with the Lord on Mount Sinai in Exodus 3 is quite fascinating as we see that any place the Lord dwells becomes hallowed.

Additionally, we gain a sense of the magnificent importance of holiness when we see how the priests of old were required to go through careful and precise procedures. Only the High Priests were especially sanctified and purified to be able to enter through the veil of the Tabernacle into the Holy of Holies once a year and offer a sacrifice unto the Lord on behalf of the people of Israel (Leviticus 21:8).

God also chose Israel because of His love for them, and He set them apart to be different from other nations (Leviticus 20:26), so that in Him, Israel would be a model nation to others of how to live and walk with the Lord. For Israel, holiness was to be their distinct witness that separated them from the unbelieving world and its way of living – to point them toward a great and loving God who calls mankind into an intimate covenantal relationship with Himself.

The Greek and Hebrew definitions of holiness are *sanctification, consecration, set apart* and *purification*. Throughout the Bible, we see how God makes distinct comparisons between those who are holy and those who are unholy. When we think about holiness, we should associate it with a person or thing that has been *chosen by the Lord*. Having received the free gift of salvation, a believing woman is charged to live a life of holiness and consecration – away from the world and unto the Lord, because her association with Jesus Christ makes her holy.

When we look at the New Testament, we see how God does a new thing with the Church, and how He calls us out to be holy before Him (2 Corinthians 7:1). Just like circumcision of the heart, the outward observances are intended to point to a deeper spiritual meaning because inward holiness matters to God, and He is concerned that we be holy in every area of our hearts.

I understood this more clearly during the countdown to my wedding, when the Lord used marriage as an illustration to demonstrate how He has selected me to be in an everlasting covenantal relationship with Himself. He has called me to a standard of holiness, and He will prepare me for this.

During the careful wedding preparations, I was reminded that my Lord is my Bridegroom – the One who has set His affection upon me and who has pledged His faithfulness and commitment to me. He is the one who has paid the price for my life, and so it is to Him that I serve and honour in return. Before I was to know a man, the Lord desired and still desires to be the intimate Lover of my soul.

Like Gomer, I too stray at times, but His love and desire for me to be set apart and prepared for Him are relentless. I knew then that whatever I experience on earth, as wonderful as it will be, is but a mere shadow of the true holy relationship that God has called me into. Just as my husband saw and chose me, The Lord has set His eyes upon me and chosen me to be His – to be set apart as *His* bride for *His* pleasure.

During the months of preparation for my wedding, I was gently convicted and reminded that I wasn't to neglect the habit of preparing for my heavenly King, but to remain keenly sensitive to the Holy Spirit as He seeks to perform the sanctifying and purifying work within me.

Holiness is not a call to perfection, but to single-mindedness, single-heartedness, sincerity and loving intentionality towards God. It is interesting to note that in the Old Testament, special holy places (such as tabernacles and temples) were set apart for God and His people to come together; now, we have the privilege of this holy place not being in a building, but *within our very hearts*. The location may have changed, but this unique characteristic of God and its outworking in our lives as believers has not.

God does not call us to a love that is rooted in selfishness, but rather, His self-giving faithfulness *compels* us to draw nearer to Him and love Him even more. As we do, our lives will naturally bear witness to His holiness as we are transformed to love the things that He loves and hate what He hates.

Holiness was never meant to be a spiritual bludgeon that flattens and squeezes the life out of our faith, and it goes beyond a rigid set of boundaries and rules. A stand of being set apart for God means that our lives serve as the embodiment and witness of God's intention for the world – in marriage, singleness, homemaking, conduct in the workplace and most importantly, in the development of our characters into the image of Christ.

THE ECHOES OF *YOUR* HEART

- *What are some of the ways that you sense God calling you toward holiness? Is this important to you?*
- *Would you be willing to put away everything that is displeasing to God and allow Him to raise you up to a standard of holiness?*

A CALL TO ACTION

The topic of holiness will always need to address the sin and waywardness in our lives.

- If there is any sin in your life, bring it to the feet of Jesus in repentance and ask Him to show you His standard of holiness.

THE ECHOES OF HER HEART

The way to wholeness is through no other avenue but the path of brokenness, where we willingly surrender all that we are to the One who knows us best.

19.
A RESTORED, WHOLE AND HEALED HEART

For she said to herself, "If only I may touch His garment, I shall be made well."

-Matthew 9:21

We end this book with a befitting chapter: the restoration of a woman's heart. Throughout the book, we have looked at the different matters of the heart of a woman – the heart's physical and spiritual function, its purpose, a broken heart, a deceitful heart, a healed, surrendered, circumcised and sensitive heart.

What does the word *restoration* mean for you?

For me, it speaks of a *reviving* and a *rebuilding* of something back into its original state or something better. It means hope. Hope that what was once dead can indeed come back to life and be established completely in the Lord- *with nothing missing.*
Luke 8:43-48 is a wonderful demonstration of a woman made whole by Jesus after suffering with a sickness in her body for

12 years. She had spent all of her money and energy on physicians, and all her efforts had proven to be futile, until one day, she met Jesus among a crowd. Hoping to be very discreet in her actions, she assembled all the strength she could, and edged closer to Him. She had faith that He could heal her if only she could touch the hem of His garment. Courageously moving forward to do so, she received instant healing in her body! What a powerful narrative and example for us to meditate on.

When a woman's heart is restored, it demonstrates not only a spiritual awakening to her Maker and His total involvement and interest in her life, but also her acceptance of His salvation offered, which grants forgiveness of her sins and the opportunity to walk in a right relationship with her Lord. When grace is released into a woman's heart, healing takes place as she begins to trust in and experience the complete sovereignty of her Lord. However, before we reach this place, we must be willing to commit to the intentional act of moving nearer to God.

I don't know about you, but I have noticed that in my own journey, I have often found myself longing to reach the reality of wholeness quite quickly! However, in order to taste of the sweet fruit of true spiritual, mental and emotional wholeness, we must be willing to allow God to take us on a bitter, and at times, difficult (but necessary) journey of pruning and development. The way to wholeness is through no other avenue but the path of brokenness, where we willingly surrender all that we are to the One who knows us best. *Without brokenness before Jesus, we cannot be put back together in Him.*

It is far easier to talk about revival with others and feel the freeing and jubilant effects of breakthrough; however, what I have learnt over the years, is that we cannot *meet* God in revival until we meet Him in our darkness and utter place of need, just like the woman in Luke 8:43-48. Until we allow Him into the places that no man has access – the places that we are afraid to unveil to others – we cannot be made whole. He must be granted permission to enter behind the veil of the masks that we put on.

"I'm okay." "I'm good."

These phrases can be so well-rehearsed and mastered that they conceal what lies within, but until we allow our hearts to be touched by Jesus, we will not come away rejoicing like the woman who had the issue of blood.

What the passage in Luke teaches me is that there is *virtue* in everything that belongs to Christ, and so by a woman's association with Him, all of His virtues flow into her heart, causing her to be sanctified each day as she seeks Him for strength, nourishment, wisdom and guidance in life (Psalm 32:8).

Consider Ezekiel 36 and 37 where God is having a dialogue with Ezekiel who is standing before a valley of dry bones. In Chapter 37, God instructs Ezekiel to prophesy over the bones for them to come back together, and Ezekiel obeys. As he speaks, the dry bones are slowly but surely revived and formed piece by piece. God then instructs Ezekiel to prophesy *life* into those bones so that they would come alive, and as Ezekiel obeys, an army that was once dead is completely restored.

God used this experience to show Ezekiel how Israel felt at that time- dead, broken and without hope. Through Ezekiel, He was demonstrating that by His power and at His command, He was able to, and indeed *willing* to renew Israel back to their former state, before their sin and rebellion.

Bringing this passage closer to our own lives, I am greatly

encouraged and humbled, because this is exactly what God wants to do within our own hearts. Dry bones for some of us could represent a famine in our spiritual walk, and a severing of our relationship with God because we have pulled away. You may be currently experiencing dry season after the next, struggling to reconnect to the Vine.

For others, dryness could be a result of rejection, abuse and hardships that have marred your heart and tricked you into believing that you are not worthy of restoration. You may be more acquainted with tears and sorrow rather than assurance and the warmth of love. Yet through it all, through our neglect, the abuse, mistakes, failings, losses, struggles and our sin, this scripture passage assures us that we are never far away from the Lord's healing touch. God is committed to rebuilding our broken areas, and He alone can bring such an injured heart back to life.

From our finite human perspective, dryness makes hope seem so far away, but faith in the healing touch of Jesus leaves the question of possibility to rest with God, in whom nothing is impossible. If you may be wondering if your dry bones can ever live again, the answer is yes! The Lord knows (Ezekiel 37:3). You can be made whole again, smile again and experience the joy and love of the Lord, no matter what your current situation looks like.

No matter how low in the valley you are or have been, you are not beyond the command of God's voice which has the power to bring about your restoration. *Even in the midst of death!* Nothing is beyond God's ability to rebuild, repair and restore.

We are all consumed by a hunger for deep and meaningful relationship, and a woman whose heart has been restored unto her Maker understands that it is only He, the true Lover of her soul, who makes her right in every way. In her weaknesses, strengths, victories, doubts and concerns about her future, she

A RESTORED, WHOLE AND HEALED HEART

knows that it is God to whom her life ultimately belongs.

Believing women are Christ's daughters, as He becomes their ultimate Father who cares for all their needs. When a woman's heart is restored, the spiritual healing that takes place realigns her to her divinely-appointed disposition, and she no longer needs to clamber for attention, nor does her life function at the sound of others' approval. Jesus has treated her spiritual infirmity indefinitely, and He continues to be her present help in times of need. *This is the hope upon which she stands and builds her life.*

When our hearts are restored, we gain ever-increasing clarity on the truth that Jesus Christ is our Prophet, Priest and King, and upon our acceptance of this, we are able to lovingly surrender our hearts to be ruled, taught and led by Him.

As restoration is realised, we understand that we are not orphans. We have great purpose, because a God that would call us to know Him would have a reason behind desiring us to know Him, and that sets us on the lifelong journey of learning, growing and blossoming at His leading. When we fully walk in this, we need never again feel the urge to fill our moments with empty void-fillers, because we will be consumed with the love that our Bridegroom has for us, and us for Him.

And indeed, what a freeing place to find ourselves in.

For of Him and through Him and to Him are all things, to whom be glory forever. Amen.

- ROMANS 11:36

***

I see the restoration of biblical womanhood

I see women walking on God's path. Strong, beautiful, broken, humbled, focused and fixated on the One who has called them into His Kingdom.

I see young women rising from the pits of darkness, pain, rejection, heartache and sin to claim their new lives in Christ – walking towards restoration with hearts wide open for God to have His way in them.

I see women shunning the ways of our times to pursue and grow into the full stature of Christ – abandoning all that they have known in the world, and running towards their Saviour in complete surrender, for complete Lordship.

I see a revival in this generation from a company of feminine hearts, unified in worship. It brings healing, breakthrough and awakens hearts to experience and make manifest the glory of God.

***

Printed in Poland
by Amazon Fulfillment
Poland Sp. z o.o., Wrocław